50 Best Memory

METHODS AND TESTS

*Work out in the
Memory Gymnasium*

50 Best Memory
METHODS AND TESTS

Work out in the Memory Gymnasium

BY MICHEL DANSEL

foulsham

LONDON • NEW YORK • TORONTO • SYDNEY

foulsham

The Publishing House, Bennetts Close,
Cippenham, Berkshire SL1 5AP, England.

ISBN 0-572-02282-4

Typeset in Great Britain by Typesetting Solutions, Slough, Berks.
Printed in Great Britain by St. Edmundsbury Press, Bury St. Edmunds, Suffolk.

CONTENTS

CHAPTER I

TRICKS
& Devices

The finest ship in the world never takes to sea without a life-boat on board. In the same way, the most exceptional and faultless memory, just like the most luxurious liner, sometimes needs a little help. Mnemonic methods, those one selects from the vast range that already exist and those that one creates for oneself, are there precisely to be used as a means of recall when faced with a sudden loss of memory.

The temporary mental block that occurs when one is overcome with examination nerves, when one is making a speech or is involved in a debate – or, for that matter, in any everyday situation – is not something that happens just to others. It is at moments like these that one must have one's life-boat and know how to launch it in time.

In order to retain what one does not want to forget, often the safest way – besides a good general knowledge of one's subject – is to learn a certain number of tricks or devices.

We have all used devices at school when we were young in order to remember, for example, how to spell certain words. *'I before E except after C'* is just one of many that help us spell correctly when we have a temporary lapse of memory.

Others include *'Knock off the Y and add IES'* and the sentence that ensures we spell 'necessary' correctly: *Never Eat Cake Eat Smoked Salmon And Remain Young.*

In this section there are a range of tests of varying difficulty. However those who have mastery of the areas covered or have the appropriate mnemonic keys will be able to answer the questions without hesitation.

It is really a matter – in the form of a game – of practising certain mental tricks and thus developing your own personal methods of retaining those facts that you wish to remember.

With most of the tests, there is a table for scores so that you can evaluate your performance.

ONE ANCIENT METHOD

In ancient Greece, when people settled a boundary between two fields, they brought with them a child and gave him a good spanking. The idea was to fix the contract in his mind so that he would be a sort of human land register in case the grown-ups were killed in battle. But we would not advise teachers to adopt such a procedure!

THE LOCI

In ancient times people attached great importance to 'landmarks' in order to memorise a speech. Knowing how to visualise these was believed to be the key to a good memory. Among the Romans, having a good memory was an essential part of rhetoric. An orator had to be able to make long speeches with the greatest precision. And to do that, he had to implant in his mind a series of 'places' (loci, the plural of locus, is the Latin for places).

So the orator would chose a building or rooms in a house with their various ornaments. Each of these he associated with the various images he needed to recall in his speech. So, for example, if he wanted to talk about liberty, he would mentally 'place' a bird in the square outside – or a spear if he wanted to discuss war. To jog his memory, all he had to do was to go through these 'places' in the order of his discourse and in this way he remembered, following a logical progression, the subjects he wanted to cover.

This theory of 'places' was developed by various writers, notably Cicero. And herein lies the origin of the expression 'in the first place'.

NINETEENTH CENTURY LITERATURE

This exercise consists of checking whether you remember English writers of the 19th century. All you have to do is put the name of a writer, poet or philosopher of this great period in each of the ten spaces given. The object is not particularly to test your literary knowledge. It is in no way a question of 'culture' in the strict sense of the term, but more a way of measuring your ability to recall names that you know but which are perhaps buried deep in your memory.

Even if you are not necessarily familiar with their works, you will inevitably have come across the names of these people in one context or another. In order to come up with many more that ten, you would probably have to delve deep into your store of knowledge.

If the names do not come to mind instantly, then you have lost the 'key' to this store and have no magic formula to help you. If you had, then you would be in a position to fill in the table with the minimum of effort.

You have three minutes to complete the exercise. Score two points for each correct answer.

YOUR ANSWERS

Nineteenth century writers	Score
1. Dickens	
2. Shakespare	
3. Jules Verne.	
4. Jerome Kdens	
5. Austen	
6.	
7.	
8.	
9.	
10.	
Total (out of 20)	

Answers on page 12

Possible answers for evaluation

1. Charlotte Brontë
2. Robert Browning
3. Lord Byron
4. John Keats
5. Thomas Hardy
6. Robert Louis Stevenson
7. Alfred Tennyson
8. William Thackeray
9. William Wordsworth
10. Charles Dickens

MEMORY AND MNEMONIC METHODS

In Greek mythology, Mnemosynis was a Titan, one of the six daughters of Uranus (who personified the Sky) and Gaia (the Earth). She personified Memory (memoria in Latin).

Mnemonic methods are techniques that everyone can use for helping their memory. They consist of converting information into images or of finding a simple formula for retention through analogy or phonetic or visual comparisons.

You invent a relationship or association between something you want to remember and something that is already firmly fixed in your mind, like your date of birth for example.

Answer analysis

1. The names given here are, of course, just a selection of

possible correct answers. There are many more nineteenth century writers you could have included. If yours are not on the list, check with a reference book before you penalise yourself too hastily with a zero score.

2. Those who instantly fill up the ten spaces without resorting to any tricks are rare. They will usually be students of literature or those particularly well-read and acquainted with that particular period. On the other hand, those who could find ten names within the time allowed, without hesitating or having to think too hard, must have had recourse to some mnemonic method.

3. Here is a mnemonic device to ensure that you are not taken unawares and find yourself overcome with nerves when faced with an apparently simple question, but one that could disconcert you in certain circumstances. All you have to do is remember the following sentence: Hardy Brontë lay browning by Ron Keats' and Tenny's son Thackeray, while Steven's son recited words worthy of Dickens. You will see that all the names in the list appear in the sentence, either in their actual form or phonetically.

A word of advice

Learning this sentence by heart will not, of course, make you an expert in nineteenth century literature. Such a method has its limits. However it can, in addition to enabling you to make a list, enable you to place a writer straight away in his or her correct period.

Remember

- To find the names of ten writers from the nineteenth century, remember the following sentence:

Hardy Brontë lay browning by Ron Keats and Tenny's son Thackeray, while Steven's son recited words worthy of Dickens.

ENGLISH RIVERS

Among the practical geographical exercises pupils are presented with at school is one in which they are asked to mark certain natural features on a blank map of a country. For example, they may be asked to identify the main rivers in England.

This test involves your capacity to remember eight of the major rivers in ENGLAND, not the British Isles. You certainly learned these at school and this exercise is not so much a question of testing your general knowledge as of measuring your capacity to recall 'stored' information.

Here is a list of different British rivers. Extract the ones that flow in England and list these in the spaces provided:

Severn	Tay	Foyle	Tyne
Exe	Erne	Mersey	Clyde
Mourne	Humber	Tees	Dee
Medway	Bann	Forth	Thames

You have three minutes to complete this exercise. Score two points for each correct answer.

YOUR ANSWERS

English rivers	Score
1.	
2.	
3.	
4.	
5.	
6.	
7.	
8.	
Total (out of 16)	

Answers on page 16

Answers for evaluation

1. Severn
2. Tyne
3. Exe
4. Mersey
5. Humber
6. Tees
7. Medway
8. Thames

Answer analysis

1. Unlike the previous exercise, it is not possible here to give different answers. You simply have to name the correct rivers – in any order.

2. By actually giving you the names of the English rivers, albeit mixed up with those of the rest of the British Isles, this test has been made considerably easier. With an appropriate mnemonic method, you should have been able to fill in the eight spaces with baffling speed. Without such a device, you would have had to refresh your memory.

3. If you want to use a magic formula, one of the keys to remembering facts consists of telling stories that you have made up. Remember the imagination knows no limits. The objective is to find the trick that enables you to retain the information.

4. Here is just one example of a sentence that might help you fix the major English rivers in your memory:

Seven tiny ex-mercenaries hum Bertie's tune midway themselves.

From this sentence, you can extract the following:

Seven   =   *Severn*

Tiny	=	*Tyne(y)*
Ex	=	*Exe*
Mercenaries	=	*Mersey(naries)*
Hum Bertie's	=	*Humber/Tees*
Midway	=	*Medway*
Themselves	=	*Thames(elves)*

5. Using this example, think up another sentence or story that best suits your own style and imagination.

A word of advice

In order to remember these 'trick' sentences, repeat them to yourself, in bed for example, when you are having some trouble sleeping.

Remember

• In order to remember eight main English rivers:

Seven tiny ex-mercenaries hum Bertie's tune midway themselves.

EUROPEAN UNION

This test is relatively easy. It does not require any particular knowledge and can be successfully completed without any recourse to a mnemonic method. However we all know that the obvious is the first thing we forget, particularly when we have to answer correctly against the clock.

In other words, it is not enough to know the countries that make up the European Union to be able to list them without any hesitation when required.

This question appears regularly in the course of various exams and is of topical interest.

You have three minutes to complete this exercise. Score two points for each correct answer.

YOUR ANSWERS

The 15 countries of the European Union	Score
1.	
2.	
3.	
4.	
5.	
6.	
7.	
8.	
9.	
10.	
11.	
12.	
13.	
14.	
15.	
Total (out of 30)	

Answers on page 20

Answers for evaluation
(in any order)

1.	France	9.	Denmark
2.	Italy	10.	Greece
3.	Luxembourg	11.	Sweden
4.	Austria	12.	United Kingdom
5.	Finland	13.	Ireland
6.	Germany	14.	Spain
7.	Belgium	15.	Portugal
8.	The Netherlands (Holland)		

Answer analysis

Even those who know the subject very well can easily, on the day of the exam or when it is really necessary to come up with the answer, find themselves in difficulty remembering all fifteen countries. In this case a mnemonic method can give them the support they need to rattle off the list.

The best speakers, the most conscientious students and even the top teachers can all have an off day when they cannot quote the information they know so well. One could make a comparison between memory and sailing: even the most experienced sailors are not immune to sea-sickness. One day the sea's turbulence may get the better of them. So it is essential to have access to a magic formula to overcome the problem.

For this exercise, one trick amongst many that can help is to construct a sentence that includes at least one of the syllables of the name of each country, or at least sounds sufficiently similar to serve as a reminder. So you could end up with something like:

Frankly Luke's austere finger, beholden to the greasy swede, unites our land and sport.

Of course, the sentence in itself is nonsense, but strange enough to be remembered! It works as follows:

Frankly	=	*France/Italy*
Luke's	=	*Luxembourg*
Austere	=	*Austria*
Finger	=	*Finland/Germany*
Beholden	=	*Belgium/Holland/Denmark*
Greasy	=	*Greece*
Swede	=	*Sweden*
Unites	=	*United Kingdom*
Our land	=	*Ireland*
Sport	=	*Spain/Portugal*

It is up to you to find your own sentence or other device which can work as a key to remembering the fifteen countries.

Remember

- In order to remember the fifteen member countries of the European Union:

Frankly Luke's austere finger, beholden to the greasy swede, unites our land and sport.

THE COMMON MARKET

In 1946 Winston Churchill launched the idea of the United States of Europe. In 1950 a French economist, Jean Monnet and the French Foreign Affairs Minister Robert Schuman proposed a common policy between France and West Germany for coal and steel production.

This was the first step towards a common economic market. The basis of the original community – France, West Germany, Belgium, Italy, Luxembourg and the Netherlands – was established in 1951. In 1973 Denmark, the United Kingdom and Ireland joined and Greece followed in 1981. Spain and Portugal joined in 1986 and the recent addition of Austria, Finland and Sweden makes fifteen members of what is now known as the European Union.

THE PHILOSOPHERS' GARDEN

This test is a little more difficult than the previous ones. It includes on the one hand Greek philosophers and on the other the difference between the leaves of the beech and hornbeam trees. While one may well know all about Greek philosophers, one's knowledge of trees may not be quite so comprehensive.

The section relating to Greek philosophers – Plato, Aristotle and Socrates – consists of ticking the proposition you believe correctly states who was influenced by whom. You have six possibilities, but you will only have to put three ticks, since each proposition has its opposite.

The section relating to the trees offers four propositions but, equally, you only have to tick two of them.

Simply tick those propositions you believe to be correct, which will be five out of the possible ten.

With the philosophers, be careful. There is a slight trap which some will avoid without problem. Those who have some helpful mnemonic keys for answering the questions instantly and easily will obviously be at an advantage.

You have three minutes to tick the five correct propositions. Score two points for each correct answer.

YOUR ANSWERS

	Reply	Score
1. *Aristotle was influenced by Plato*		
2. *Aristotle was influenced by Socrates*		
3. *Socrates was influenced by Plato*		
4. *Socrates was influenced by Aristotle*		
5. *Plato was influenced by Socrates*		
6. *Plato was influenced by Aristotle*		
7. *The beech leaf has bristles*		
8. *The beech leaf is serrated*		
9. *The hornbeam leaf has bristles*		
10. *The hornbeam leaf is serrated*		
Total (out of 20)		

Answers on page 24

Answers for evaluation

The propositions that you should have ticked as being correct are:

| 1 | 2 | 5 | 7 | 10 |

Answer analysis

1. Plato was the disciple of Socrates and Aristotle was the disciple of Plato. But the trap is that, through the teachings he received from Plato, Aristotle was influenced by the doctrine of Socrates.

2. The beech leaf is oval and has bristles underneath, while the leaf of the hornbeam is serrated with pointed double 'teeth'.

3. In order to place the three Greek philosophers in their correct chronological order – and that of influence – remember the word *spa*, which uses their initials.

4. There is a simple way of not confusing the leaves of the beech and the hornbeam trees. Just remember the magic sentence: *The bristly beech points to the hornbeam.*

Remember

- To put the philosophers in their correct chronological and influential order, remember the word *spa* – made up of their initials.

- To remember the difference between the leaves of the beech and the hornbeam: *The bristly beech points to the hornbeam.*

THE GREAT GREEK PHILOSOPHERS

We know very little about Socrates (470-399 BC). As he did not write anything, it is principally to Plato that we owe the development of his doctrine, despite the efforts of Zenophon to belittle him. Plato was twenty when he met Socrates and he spent eight years close to him. The teachings of the master, whose wisdom was considered unrivalled, were confined to conversations and speeches. He was the founder of western philosophy. In search of justice and truth, he knew how to introduce into the most simple discussions an extraordinary moral dimension. His motto was: 'Know yourself'.

As for Plato (427-347 BC), he could be considered as the founder of western philosophical *writing*. His works took the form of dialogues in which his master Socrates, to whom he was deeply attached, figured as the principal speaker. Plato exercised his influence on Aristotle (384-322 BC), who imprinted largely his mark on European thought. In effect it was Aristotle who, in the Middle Ages and also during the Renaissance period, was considered the point of reference. He symbolised all the knowledge of the Ancient Greeks and was regarded as the real creator of the sciences of anatomy and physiology, as well as logic. One of the greatest intellectual minds in of all time, Aristotle was influenced in part of his philosophical thinking by his master Plato. As for his peripateticism (from the Greek *peripatein*, to walk around talking), he was linking himself with one of the Socratic traditions.

POST-WAR AMERICAN PRESIDENTS

Since the end of the Second World War (1945) there have been ten presidents of the United States. The following exercise, still related to mnemonic methods, consists of naming them, preferably in chronological order although this is not essential. The important thing is to be able to list them all.

You have five minutes to name your ten presidents. Score two points for each correct answer.

YOUR ANSWERS

The post-war American presidents	Score
1.	
2.	
3.	
4.	
5.	
6.	
7.	
8.	
9.	
10.	
Total (out of 20)	

Answers on page 28

Answers for evaluation

The following, in chronological order, are the ten presidents of the United States since the end of the Second World War:

Harry Truman (1945-52)

Dwight Eisenhower (1953-60)

John F Kennedy (1961-63)

Lyndon Johnson (1963-68)

Richard Nixon (1969-74)

Gerald Ford (1974-76)

Jimmy Carter (1977-80)

Ronald Reagan (1981-88)

George Bush (1989-92)

Bill Clinton (1993 –)

Answer analysis

1. This test is not easy, unless you have some trick for remembering the names. Alternatively, you can use the method of association, where you link each with important events or with something they were involved with that was of historical or other importance. One would almost certainly remember, for example, that Dwight Eisenhower led the Allied Forces in the final overthrow of Hitler, John Kennedy was assassinated in Dallas and Richard Nixon fell to the Watergate scandal. Also that Jimmy Carter was known as the 'Peanut President' and Ronald Reagan was a former film star.

2. Among the formulae which might enable you to recall the list of presidents most easily, here is one that takes the

form of a sentence, playing with phonetics: *True ice Kenjo nicks for car-ray buckling.* This is, of course, basically gibberish, but silly enough to be remembered. And that's the whole point. To spell it out: *True* (Truman) *ice* (Eisenhower) *Kenjo* (Kennedy/Johnson) *nicks* (Nixon) *for car-ray* (Carter/Reagan) *buckling* (Bush/Clinton).

Remember

- In order to remember the ten American presidents since the Second World War:

  True ice Kenjo nicks for car-ray buckling.

ONE IMAGE HOLDS ANOTHER

To help your memory, all the previous mnemonics are valuable only if they prove effective at the time you need them. The most important key to success lies in your ability to imagine, to hang images on situations and create points of reference.

Nowadays, with so many electronic devices available for noting down information (tape recorders, computers, video recorders, etc), we all too often lose sight of the role and importance of the memory. We ignore it and abuse it when it is to us like lava is to a volcano – that is to say, a power with the potential to change our lives.

In the ancient world, when printing was unheard of, memory was of prime importance. Without it, the orator could not make his speech. For the Romans, there were two kinds of images: the first concerned 'words' and the second 'objects'. They were used to recall arguments, ideas or things. For the student of rhetoric, objects represented the subject of the discourse and words its language.

While the image was commonly used by all Roman authors, who were greatly inspired by the Greeks, some of them even went as far as supporting the idea of creating images strong enough to cause emotional shocks in order to improve their retention.

All this work amounted to some real mental gymnastics, which called on motivation, concentration and self-discipline.

This test is based on methods of memorising which will be well-known to some and less known – or even completely new – to others. But its importance does not lie there. What really matters is to activate your mind in such a way that you can produce, in whatever situation, your own set of formulae which will act as the lifeline for your memory if this suddenly fails you at a critical moment.

You have one minute for this test. Score two points for each correct answer.

YOUR ANSWERS

		Y/N	Score
1.	*Finland is a Scandinavian country*		
2.	*Port is on the right*		
3.	*The history of Mesopotamia is linked with the Tigris and Euphrates*		
4.	*The word* **embarrass** *is spelt with two Rs*		
5.	*In maths, + x - = +*		
6.	*The ratio between the circumference and the diameter is 3.1415926535*		
7.	*Domitian was the last of the Twelve Caesars*		
8.	*The pneumo-gastric is a cranial nerve*		
9.	*Mercury is the nearest planet to the Sun*		
10.	*Ramsgate is one of the Cinque Ports*		
	Total (out of 20)		

Answers on page 32

Answers for evaluation

1. **No.** Finland is not a Scandinavian country.

2. **No.** Port is not on the right.

3. **Yes.** The history of Mesopotamia is linked with the Tigris and the Euphrates.

4. **Yes.** The word embarrass is spelt with two Rs.

5. **No.** In maths, $+ \text{ x } -$ does not equal $+$.

6. **Yes.** The ratio between the circumference and the diameter is 3.1415926535.

7. **Yes.** Domitian was the last of the Twelve Caesars.

8. **Yes.** The pneumo-gastric is a cranial nerve.

9. **Yes.** Mercury is the nearest planet to the Sun.

10. **No.** Ramsgate is not one of the Cinque Ports.

Answer analysis

1. This test, as you have obviously already realised, has no theme, which makes it more difficult for some and easier for others. Those who are not particularly keen on, for example, history or geography still have the chance to exercise their memory in other areas. On the other hand, those who are only interested in say, astrology, and use their memory for nothing else (which is highly unlikely) will find themselves heavily handicapped by this set of questions.

2. Those who have magical formulae for answering correctly will have doubtless completed the test in less than thirty seconds.

3. What are the mnemonic keys that will enable you to provide the right answers without any hesitation?

Question 1

In spite of what certain books might say, geographically Finland is not part of Scandinavia. On the other hand, from an economic, social and cultural point of view, there is a Nordic council made up of Sweden, Norway, Denmark, Iceland and Finland. From a linguistic point of view, Finnish belongs to the Balto-Finnish group of Finno-Ugrian languages and is in no way connected with the Scandinavian languages. Scandinavia is made up of three countries: Sweden, Norway and Denmark. To remember this, there is a key: **145**. In the word *Scandinavia,* the first letter is an S (Sweden), the fourth an N (Norway) and the fifth a D (Denmark). There is no F (Finland).

Question 2

Facing the prow (or front end) of a boat, port is on the left and starboard is on the right. One way of remembering this is that P (as in port) comes before S (as in starboard) and L (left) comes before R (right). Another way you might find helpful is that starboard contains two Rs – doubly right!

Question 3

Both the Tigris and Euphrates rivers played a determining role in the history of Mesopotamia (now Iraq) on both a strategic and cultural level, as well as having a catastrophic effect due to flooding. So the two rivers, which share the same mouth (in the Persian Gulf) are both linked to the history of Mesopotamia. The following simple sentence might help you remember them: *In Iraq the tiger makes you afraid*.

Question 4

The word *embarrass* has two Rs. One way of remembering this is to think how red you go with it (i.e. more than one R). Another way is to think of doubling letters – two Rs and two Ss.

Question 5

This is wrong. + x − = −. Here is a good old method of making sure you get your plusses and minuses right.

The friends of my friends are my friends (thus + x + = +)
The friends of my enemies are my enemies (thus + x − = −)
The enemies of my friends are my enemies (thus − x + = −)
The enemies of my enemies are my friends (thus − x − = +)

Question 6

This is correct. The ratio between the circumference of a circle and its diameter is 3.1415926535, also known as pi. One way to remember this is to break up the numbers, such as 31-41-592-65-35, so that you retain them as a kind of jingle. You could also create a sentence, where the letters comprising each word correspond with the numbers. So: *How (3) I (1) mark (4) a (1) round (5) formation (9) by (2) using (6) radii (5) and (3) rings (5).*

Question 7

Domitian is certainly the last of the 'Twelve Caesars', an expression taken from the work of the Roman historian Suetonus (AD 75-160) for designating Julius Caesar and the eleven Roman emperors who succeeded him. The list, in chronological order, is: Caesar, Augustus, Tiberius, Caligula, Claudius, Nero, Galba, Otho, Vitellius, Vespasian, Titus and Domitian. One of the best known ways of remembering them all is to learn by heart the following triplet, which contains the first syllable of each name in the correct order: *Caeautica Claunegalo Vivestido*

Question 8

This is correct. The pneumo-gastric is one of the twelve cranial nerves. Here is the full list of them: olfactive, optic, common ocular motor, pathetic, trigeminal, external ocular motor, facial, auditory, glosso-pharyngeal, pneumo-gastric, spinal and hypoglossal. Although not the kind of information one would normally keep on the tip of one's tongue, for medical students it is necessary to remember such information. One way is through devising a sentence in which each word starts with the first letter of each of the nerves. So one could have: *Out of common practice the expert finds a good plaster stops haemorrhages.*

Question 9

This is correct. Mercury is the planet nearest to the Sun. In order of their proximity to the Sun, the nine principal planets are: Mercury, Venus, Earth, Mars, Jupiter, Saturn, Uranus, Neptune and Pluto. To remember this list, you simply have to make up a sentence you will easily remember, in which the first letter of each word corresponds to the first letter of each planet. For example: *My vicar enjoys making jokey sermons using naughty pictures.*

Question 10

This is incorrect. Ramsgate is not one of the Cinque Ports. These are a group of sea-ports in the South East of England which in olden days provided the major part of the Navy and were in return given certain important privileges. The original five (hence *Cinque*) were Dover, Hastings, Hythe, Romney and Sandwich, which were later joined by Rye and Winchelsea. One way of remembering the names of the seven ports is through the following sentence: *Over-hasty Hyrom forgets which is the right winch.* This takes in key syllables and uses phonetics to introduce all the ports.

Exercises

Make up your own magical formula or device for remembering different facts, information and names, based on the principles given here. For example, who are the current members of the Commonwealth? Can you name all the Socialist Prime Ministers? How many pints are there in a litre – or pounds in a kilo?

WORDS AND NUMBERS

In order to memorise numbers – and before creating your own code – it would be helpful to familiarise yourself with some of the methods which already exist.

In our society, numbers occupy an increasingly important place. Each of us carries around a considerable quantity of numbers. For practical reasons, there are some we need to remember, such as our own and other people's telephone numbers, our bank card code and our National Health number. In particular, it is vital to remember the burglar alarm stop code, useful to have the bank account number to hand and advisable to know the birthdays of relatives and close friends. There are doubtless many more. Equally, it can be helpful to have some historical references and to know certain dates connected with our studies, our particular interests, our research, our social life and so on.

The method involved in this test is a variant of that developed in the seventeenth century by Henry Herdson. It involves linking a word to each number so that an image can be planted in our brain. The exercise here is to memorise the following list and then to sort out the words that correspond to the numbers given in the ten questions:

1	=	pencil	6	=	cube
2	=	shoes	7	=	curve
3	=	triangle	8	=	glasses
4	=	square	9	=	magnifying glass
5	=	hand	0	=	orange

You can then use the code to make up a short sentence using these words. For example:

82 = glasses – shoes

You could make up the following sentences using these two words: *"My glasses are in my shoes"* or *"I put on my glasses to find my shoes"*.

655 = cube – hand – hand

Your sentence could be: *"I take a cube in both hands"*.

9123 = magnifying glass – pencil – shoes – triangle
Your sentence could be: *"I take my magnifying glass and my pencil, I change shoes and I draw a triangle"*.

You have four minutes to memorise the above list and then five minutes to decode the ten sets of numbers and write down the relevant words. Score two points for each correct set of words.

YOUR ANSWERS

Corresponding words	Score
1. 45	
2. 17	
3. 908	
4. 642	
5. 901	
6. 3189	
7. 9628	
8. 5503	
9. 11528	
10. 92634	
Total (out of 20)	

Answers on page 38

THE ORIGINAL CODE

The code devised by Henry Herdson does not correspond exactly to the one we have used here, except for the
numbers 5, 8, 9 and 0, which we have not altered. His 1,
for example, was a candle – a common and indispensable object before the days of electricity. The 3 was a tri-
dent, a three-pronged fork of an earlier age. As for the 7,
this was a 'cut-throat' razor now generally only used in
very old fashioned hairdressing salons.

Answers for evaluation

1. square – hand
2. pencil – curve
3. magnifying glass – orange – glasses
4. cube – square – shoes
5. magnifying glass – orange – pencil
6. triangle – pencil – glasses – magnifying glass
7. magnifying glass – cube – shoes – glasses
8. hand – hand – orange – triangle
9. pencil – pencil – hand – shoes – glasses
10. magnifying glass – shoes – cube – triangle – square

Answer analysis

1. Five minutes to decode all the numbers is quite a long
    time, but you will probably need most of this to begin
    with until your code becomes so familiar you can
    almost sing it like a musical scale. You need to learn it by
    heart and practise it for a few minutes each day to gain
    the maximum benefit.

2. It is noticeable that this method becomes more com-
    plicated after three numbers.

3. This code is only an example, of course. You can create
    your own, using any objects of your choice.

4. If you need to store the coded numbers for any length of time, do not hesitate to make up a sentence using all the numbers (and hence words) and repeat it morning and evening, at least for the first few days, until it is firmly fixed in your mind.

Remember

To remember numbers with words:

- Take time to learn and familiarise yourself well with a code of corresponding numbers and words.

- Continually practise to convert numbers into words.

- Put your imagination to work and create sentences using the words that 'translate' the numbers.

LETTERS FOR NUMBERS

Among the methods that exist for remembering numbers, there is one that is highly regarded in the realm of mnemonics. It is that of a certain Abbé Moigno (1804-1884) who used consonants to represent numbers. His work has inspired numerous memory specialists.

The procedure, which is easy to grasp, has the merit of being highly effective.

Here, among other variations, is a list of possible 'codes':

1 = t (for its vertical line which resembles the 1)
2 = n (for its two 'legs')
3 = m (for its three 'legs')
4 = l (in its capital form it resembles the 4)
5 = s (for its resemblance)
6 = b (for its resemblance)
7 = r (by symmetry)
8 = f (because of its two loops when hand-written)
9 = g (for its resemblance)
0 = c (for its resemblance, plus if you put two Cs together with one inverted they form an O)

This method calls on one's imagination and perspicacity. The object is to use the consonants to make up a word in order to remember a number.

For example: 42 = l and n. The question to ask is what word should one use that contains these two consonants but none of the others in the coded list? One possible answer is lion.

Take another example: 978 = g, r, f. One possible answer is grief.

You have ten minutes to familiarise yourself with the above coded list and memorise it. Then allow yourself ten more minutes to make up a word or a sentence from your date of birth and your bank account number.

The following test consists of finding a word or building up a phrase or sentence from the ten numbers given, which you must first decode.

You have ten minutes to complete this test. Score two points for each correct answer.

YOUR ANSWERS

	Words or phrases	Score
1.	*41*	
2.	*68*	
3.	*49*	
4.	*93*	
5.	*344*	
6.	*4029*	
7.	*2171*	
8.	*7164*	
9.	*52012*	
10.	*46717*	
	Total (out of 20)	

Answers on page 42

Answers for evaluation

1. $41 = l - t =$ lit

2. $68 = b - f =$ beef

3. $49 = l - g =$ leg

4. $93 = g - m =$ gym

5. $344 = m - l - l =$ mill

6. $4029 = l - c - n - g =$ lacing

7. $2171 = n - t - r - t =$ notoriety

8. $7164 = r - t - b - l =$ rateable

9. $52012 = s - n - c - t - n =$ since then

10. $46717 = l - b - r - t - r =$ laboratory

Answer analysis

1. When making up a word or phrase from the decoded letters, it is perfectly possible to use any letters not included in the coded list. For example, for *4029* you could use the word *licking* since *k* does not count as part of the code. And with *52012* the letter *h* has been included in the word *then*. You can see how this method allows you to use your imagination. It demands simply that you respect the code, but leaves the door open for your own fantasies.

2. Here again, to make this method work, it is imperative to practise in order to master the procedure.

3. You can, of course, make up your own code. But this one has the advantage of being logical and easy to memorise.

Remember

To learn how to retain numbers with letters:

- Familiarise yourself with a code (that proposed or one of your choice) and practise converting numbers into letters.

- The code of consonants, which relies on a simple logical procedure, has already proved itself. It works through analogy, resemblance and correspondence and, furthermore, it has the merit of being easy to retain.

- Learn to convert numbers into consonants and consonants into words spontaneously.

HOW TO CREATE REFERENCE POINTS

In order to make up your own reference points to help you remember facts, figures or information, there are three basic possibilities:

1. Rely on existing methods.
2. Adapt existing methods.
3. Invent your own methods.

- There is no universal manual on mnemonic methods in which you can find a miraculous formula for remembering everything you want.

- You must learn to adapt the existing methods according to your requirements.

- On the chessboard of your memory, imagination often represents the master piece.

- Learning to remember is learning to discipline your thinking on a daily basis.

- Learning to remember is being in a permanent state of alert, on the least occasions, to activate your mental capacity not to forget.

- Learning to remember is a discipline requiring constant effort and an ever-lively imagination.

- A major key here is:

  MOTIVATION + ACTION = SUCCESS

- When learning to remember, all methods are good ones. Only the result counts. But you should not exclude those that already exist.

There are a number of different methods you can use to memorise a text without any problem. If it is a rhyming

poem, the play of similar sounds at the end of each line or verse helps you remember it.

There is the traditional method which consists of learning the lines two at a time, repeating them and then moving on to the next two after the first two have been memorised. That follows for any text one wants to learn by heart.

Learning in the evening seems to be the most effective, since it provides the best recall of knowledge the following day.

For some, this method of 'horizontal' memorising is enough. But there is always an element of risk that one still might forget. To ensure that this does not happen, you need to support it with a 'vertical' reference. This will enable you to avoid that famous 'hole' in the memory, or the confusion which prevents you from finding the beginning of the next verse.

In fact, it is much easier to remember the rhymes than the first words of each line. You therefore need to create a link so that you do miss anything out.

For an example, we will take William Wordsworth's well-known poem *I wandered lonely as a cloud . . .*, which he wrote in 1807.

I wandered lonely as a cloud
That floats on high o'er vales and hills,
When all at once I saw a crowd,
A host, of golden daffodils;
Beside the lake, beneath the trees,
Fluttering and dancing in the breeze.

Continuous as the stars that shine
And twinkle on the milky way,
They stretched in never-ending line
Along the margin of the bay:
Ten thousand saw I at a glance,
Tossing their heads in sprightly dance.

The waves beside them danced; but they
Out-did the sparkling waves in glee:
A poet could not but be gay,
In such a jocund company:
I gazed – and gazed – but little thought
What wealth the show to me had brought:

For oft, when on my couch I lie
In vacant or in pensive mood,
They flash upon that inward eye
Which is the bliss of solitude;
And then my heart with pleasure fills,
And dances with the daffodils.

Having started by learning the poem using the 'horizontal' method, concentrate on trying to retain the first word or two of each line. Thus:

I wandered
That floats
When all
A host
Beside the
Fluttering

Continuous
And twinkle
They stretched
Along the
Ten thousand
Tossing their

The waves
Out-did
A poet
In such
I gazed
What wealth

For oft
In vacant
They flash
Which is
And then
And dances

The advantages of this 'vertical' method of memorising a poem are:

1. The beginning of a line leads into the rest in an almost automatic way.

2. These words make up a sort of relay, a logical link-up which is indispensable for remembering poems that much better. Any text that has lost its logic, poem or otherwise, is difficult or even impossible to remember.

3. One can compare text to a piece of cloth where the threads that make it up run both horizontally and vertically.

4. To be sound, the memory should take in both the horizontal and vertical references.

With a piece of prose, in addition to learning horizontally, you should also remember the first two words of each sentence.

There is a classic method for remembering numbers which consists of associating them with words that sound similar. You could, for example, use the following code:

one	=	bun
two	=	shoe
three	=	tree
four	=	floor
five	=	alive
six	=	sticks
seven	=	heaven

eight	=	late
nine	=	fine
zero	=	Zorro

It is up to you to make up the code that you are most likely to remember. There is no point in creating artificial reference points with which you are not familiar. Use words that you use regularly in your daily or professional life.

For example, if you are a keen gardener or have a particular interest in plants and vegetables, you could devise a code like the one below:

one	=	onion
two	=	tulip
three	=	pea
four	=	forsythia
five	=	chive
six	=	salix
seven	=	cedar
eight	=	potato
nine	=	lime
zero	=	azalea

This example may appear difficult and quite inaccessible to all those who are not familiar which such names. However it will be all too obvious for those who have a genuine interest in and knowledge of gardening.

- You should create your code on the basis of an area of your knowledge which is:
  - very clear (well assimilated) and
  - familiar (which you use often).

- You should always use the same code.

- The principle of a code can be discouraging to begin with, since it requires a certain degree of mental gymnastics.

- In order to be comfortable with your code, you should play with it on every possible occasion.

- Fix those objects you have chosen for your code clearly in your mind when you associate them with their corresponding numbers.

THERE ARE OTHER METHODS

You can, of course, also associate numbers with:

- historical references,

- birth dates of people close to you,

- dates of significant events in your life,

- stereotype images (e.g. 999 for emergency calls),

- telephone or bank account numbers and so on.

For example, you have to remember the number *1039652*.

1. You could remember this number using the following references:

    10   =   the Prime Minister's London residence in Downing Street

    39   =   the start of the Second World War

    652 =   your wife's date of birth (i.e. June 1952)

2. Using these references, you can also make up a little story with any contents you like. The essential point is that it becomes indelibly fixed in your brain.

    This could be something like:

    The Prime Minister announced war with Hitler long before my wife was born.

CHAPTER II

A MAJOR KEY:
Organisation

The things we learn are not securely fixed in our memories and can disappear at any time. Each day that passes brings its crop of memories. They usually appear at random, in no special order and are totally disorganised. This is because our memories leave out numerous facts, events and aspects of our lives and knowledge, some more and some less important.

- In order to retain and be able to retrieve things you have learned, you have to organise them.

- Muddled memories are obscured, and lost over time.

- Memory and organisation are closely linked.

- Organising your memory means putting it in order.

- A disordered memory has trouble retaining the various elements of information. Consequently it is not able to retrieve them when needed.

- The order must be logical.

- Organising the memory involves regrouping, classifying and categorising.

Example

With a shopping list that contains the following: *butter, bread, dry cleaning, flour, shoe repairs,* you can regroup it into just two categories:

1. Food *(butter, bread, flour)*, reminding yourself of the fact that flour is used in making bread and that to make a cake you need flour and butter.

2. Services *(dry cleaning, shoe repairs)*.

Now you have only two categories to remember, which take in all five elements. So your memory is not over-taxed and will retain the information better.

The more developed the organisation, the more you will remember.

In this section, different tests of varying difficulty highlight the need to structure your thoughts properly to memorise that much better. They rely essentially on your ability to classify, regroup and grade, and to work out categories, groups and sub-groups.

You will in time acquire the speed necessary to reason logically in order to learn to remember. It is a question of practice.

Each test includes an evaluation so that you can assess your performance and progress.

LOGICAL CLASSIFICATION

The memory requires order and organisation. It cannot manage anything muddled or jumbled. In this respect, it is a little like a house, an office or a wardrobe. Its contents, the information it receives, must not be stored indiscriminately. You must never forget that the whole point of the memory is to be effective. And disorder is an open door for confusion and forgetting.

By being willing to structure your thoughts, you will hold all the trump cards in terms of learning how to remember. If you mix up what you are trying to memorise, your mind will be muddled and your memory will work less well.

The object of this test, as with the others in this section, is to measure your capacity for classifying, sorting and grading the information or categories into groups and sub-groups.

Let us take an example. Here are ten words to remember:

poplar	*nature*
rat	*bird*
lapwing	*tree*
rodent	*crow*
oak	*coypu*

Trying to retain these names quickly and permanently in the order in which they appear is a task doomed to failure. To give yourself the best possible chance of remembering them all, you must adopt a logical classification, order and good sense. How should you do this?

a) Look for the category: *nature*.

b) Look for the groups: *tree, bird, rodent*.

c) Look for the sub-groups: *poplar & oak, lapwing & crow, rat & coypu*.

This gives you the following chart or tree:

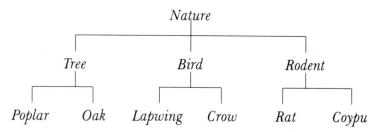

With the words thus grouped in a logical order, they can be memorised much more easily.

Organisation = effective memory

The test

Using similar principles to those in the example above, you have four minutes to put these ten words into three groups.

cenotaph	effigy
see-saw	quay
wharf	cemetery
park	pool
sand	barge

Score two points for each word correctly placed in its group.

YOUR ANSWERS

Your classification	Score
1. First group	
2. Second group	
3. Third group	
Answers on page 54 Total (out of 20)	

Note that there are three words in the first two groups and four words in the third group.

Answers for evaluation

1. Cemetery, effigy, cenotaph.

2. Quay, barge, wharf.

3. Park, pool, see-saw, sand.

Answer analysis

1. You can see that the classification of words – here into three groups – helps you to retain the ten words given. This is because one memorises things better when they are arranged in a logical fashion than when they are jumbled up.

2. The three places in the list give you three possible groups:

   cemetery + effigy + cenotaph

   quay + barge + wharf

   park + pool + see-saw + sand

3. Logical classification allows for efficient memorising. As in a well-organised house the pans are not muddled up with the clothes; one is more likely to see a barge by the quayside than in a park!

THE THEME HUNT BEGINS

Here is a list of ten words. Study them carefully and decide on the two principal themes under which the words can be grouped in sets of five:

flower

match

scent

fire

rose

flame

carrot

heat

herb

spark

This test is not difficult. It consists simply of regrouping the words in a logical way. To memorise them more easily, you are must classify the information.

You will see that there is space for just five answers. This represents one group and you are free to chose the theme you want and its corresponding five words.

You have one minute to list your five words. Score two points for each correct answer.

Make certain that you don't look at the answers before you do the test!

YOUR ANSWERS

	Themes	Score
1.		
2.		
3.		
4.		
5.		
	Total (out of 10)	

Answers on page 57

A LITTLE ETYMOLOGY

Going back to origins, the Greek *memnon* means 'who remembers' and the element *mnesia is* connected with it and signifies 'memory'. Still with Greek, *mnemotikos* means 'which concerns the memory'.

The prefix *a* was used to form a negative in Greek, giving us the word amnesia, meaning 'forgetfulness'. From another very similar Greek word, *amnestia*, meaning 'forgetting (offences)', we have the word amnesty.

So you can clearly see the connection of certain words used in this book, such as mnemonic.

'Memory' comes from the Latin word *memoria*, which is linked with *memor* (who remembers) and *memoris* (who reminds).

Answers for evaluation

The two possible groups are:

1. Match, spark, flame, fire, heat.
2. Flower, rose, scent, herb, carrot.

Answer analysis

1. There are two themes:
   - Fire
   - Vegetation

2. To memorise the 'fire' group more easily, it is possible to work on a logical classification, as follows: with a *match* one creates a *spark*; the *spark* leads to a *flame*; the *flame* produces a *fire*; the *fire* gives off *heat*. As for the 'vegetation' group, there are two sub-groups, as follows:

   a) flower, rose, scent.

   b) herb, carrot.

Remember

To unravel the themes:

- Work towards logical groupings.
- Inside each theme, classify the information in order to ensure better memorising.

ONE THEME HIDES ANOTHER

Learning to structure your thinking involves a logical step requiring neither scholarship nor special knowledge. To achieve it you need to train yourself to classify, sort, arrange into categories and grade. It is the first indispensable stage before fine-tuning your analytical mind and exercising it to find the sub-themes, sub-groups and sub-sets. This work develops your logic and helps your mind to work more productively.

The following test differs from the previous ones. For a start, the list of words is a lot longer. And the aim is not to remember them but to extract from them the five principal themes, which will make up your answer – in any order. The words are:

divan	hare
may-bug	beetle
sock	jersey
armchair	kiwi
bracelet	elephant
blouse	necklace
slow-worm	wild boar
hat-stand	fig
mango	wardrobe
ring	skirt
grape	brooch

You have two minutes to identify and list the five themes. Score two points for each correct answer.

YOUR ANSWERS

Themes	Score
1.	
2.	
3.	
4.	
5.	
Total (out of 10)	

Answers on page 60

Answers for evaluation

1. furniture
2. animals
3. clothes
4. jewellery
5. fruit

Answer analysis

1. The list of *furniture* is made up of:
   divan
   armchair
   hat-stand
   wardrobe

2. The list of *animals* is made up of:
   may-bug
   slow-worm
   hare
   beetle
   elephant
   wild boar

3. The list of *clothes* is made up of:
   sock
   blouse
   jersey
   skirt

4. The list of *jewellery* is made up of:

bracelet

ring

necklace

brooch

5. The list of *fruit* is made up of:

mango

grape

kiwi

fig

6. In the list of *animals*, you can distinguish between three sub-groups or families:

   - reptiles (slow-worm)
   - insects (may-bug, beetle)
   - mammals (hare, elephant, wild boar)

Remember

To differentiate the themes:

- In the list given here, do not take *kiwi* as an animal. In other words, you must think carefully about the meanings of the words in relation to the groups.

SYLLABLES & WORDS

You should never miss the chance to put your sense of organisation to the test.

You will find below ten words broken up into syllables, which have been scattered. The test consists of rearranging the syllables in a logical order to restore the ten words – just like a jigsaw puzzle. Like the pieces of a jigsaw, each syllable can only be used once.

Example

| ta | mo | ca | ni | har | ble |

From these syllables, you can make up the words *table* and *harmonica*.

Study all the syllables in the following list carefully before starting to assemble words. This way you will hopefully avoid the risk of mistakes.

da	a	cha	clo
fai	sti	cla	ri
ve	che	ne	ling
tin	ti	li	sin
ge	sa	fy	cy
re	ous	ty	mor

You can consult this list of syllables while you are filling in the ten words, which can be in any order. Use a pencil so that you can rub out easily and change your words, if necessary. Remember, you can only use each syllable once.

You have ten minutes to make up the ten words. Score two points for each correct answer.

YOUR ANSWERS

Made-up word	Score
1.	
2.	
3.	
4.	
5.	
6.	
7.	
8.	
9.	
10.	
Total (out of 20)	

Answers on page 64

Answers for evaluation

1. dare
2. failing
3. live
4. satin
5. singe
6. ache
7. chastity
8. timorous
9. clarify
10. cyclone

Answer analysis

1. In such tests, there may well be alternative combinations of syllables. If you do find different words, on the same basis of using each syllable only once, then of course you should score the necessary points.

2. There are certain clues involving the above list which will help you assemble your words. For example, no word will end in *fai* and we were only able to find three obscure words in the *Shorter Oxford Dictionary* that began with *fy*, a syllable most commonly found at the end of a word, as is *ous*. Such clues should help you avoid going down any blind alleys in your search for words.

Remember

To reconstruct words with scattered syllables:

- Read the whole list carefully.
- Work successively through, trying different syllables.
- Remember to use all the syllables.

A WALK IN PARIS

Organisation very often implies a logical construction. Information thrown indiscriminately into a text only serves to confuse the reader.

Among the methods used, notably for description, deduction is the simplest. This consists in following a specific order of facts, starting with the most general and progressing to the more particular, from the broadest to the narrowest, from the overall to the detailed.

Inference works the other way round. It starts with the detail and leads through to the whole, a little like the image of concentric circles or progressively larger rings forming on the surface of the water around the same point.

This test is more complicated than the previous one because its form is different. It consists of spotting ten stages of grading in the text that follows. These stages are organised on a decreasing scale – going from the general to the particular.

Make a note, from 1 to 10, of the various stages of the description, following the order of the text.

You have one minute to study the text and complete the list of stages. Score two points for each correct answer.

The text
Overlooking Paris and its hustle and bustle, Montreuil with its steep streets and poetically undisciplined greenery revives memories of a rural life not long passed.

If we take Rue du Cher, we arrive in the stylish and very pleasant little Place Emile Landrin, encircled by houses. It is named after a town councillor of the borough (1841-1914). Here there are trees, benches and a small fountain decorated with a cherub.

Exercise
This is a question of spotting the way in which presentation of the information goes from the general to the particular, rather like an approach shot homing in on its final target.

YOUR ANSWERS

From general to specific	Score
1.	
2.	
3.	
4.	
5.	
6.	
7.	
8.	
9.	
10.	
Total (out of 20)	

Answers on page 68

Answers for evaluation

1. Paris
2. Montreuil
3. Streets
4. Rue du Cher
5. Place Emile Landrin
6. Houses
7. Trees
8. Benches
9. Small fountain
10. Cherub

Answer analysis

In the first paragraph one passes from Paris to the district of Montreuil in order to arrive in the streets that characterise this part of the capital. In the second paragraph, one sets off from one street in particular to reach a small square *(place)*, which is identified. Following this is a logically decreasing order of elements one can see, starting with the largest objects and ending with the smallest: houses, trees, benches, the small fountain and finally the cherub.

Remember

- On the question of organisation, the process of *deduction* starts with the general to finish with the particular. It is simple and logical and can be used in different areas of human activity.

- The process of *inference* flows in the opposite direction. It is the method used by the detective who starts with the detail and finishes with the whole picture.

AN EXAMPLE OF INFERENCE

In a large house there is a man who no longer answers any calls. For several days his car has stood in front of the closed door. His shutters are also closed. Concerned by this, the neighbours warn the police who arrive to investigate. They force open the door, which is locked on the inside, enter a room with a very high ceiling and discover the man hanging from a rope attached to a beam, with his feet two metres from the floor. The room is completely empty: not a ladder or any sign of a support which would have enabled the victim to reach such a height in order to hang himself. The suspicion of a crime poorly disguised as suicide seems obvious.

A young policeman, more curious than his colleagues, bent down under the unfortunate man's suspended body and put his hand on the floor. He found traces of damp which aroused his investigative senses. On looking more closely he found that a strip of floor about two metres long was significantly wet while everywhere else, all round the room, was completely dry. This anomaly led him to believe that the mystery of hanged man was to be found under his feet.

He went round the other rooms in the house in search of clues, and this initiative was rewarded when he discovered a delivery note on which was written in very clumsy handwriting: "12 blocks of ice". He immediately called the company concerned to check on the size of the blocks they supplied. This information enabled him to reject the hypothesis of a faked suicide.

He convinced his colleagues by explaining to them that, in order to trick everybody – and perhaps his insurance company, the victim had built a staircase of ice in order to reach the rope and put it round his neck, in the hope of leaving no trace of what he had done.

This is an example of an investigation carried out by a process of inference, which involves starting with a detail to clarify the whole situation.

COMMUNICATION = ORGANISATION

A sentence only makes sense if it is organised. To ask some-one for information, you organise the words in the proper order of our language because no communication is possible without organisation.

For example, what could anyone reply to a question that was worded as follows:

"How is nearest many the station it miles to railway?"

A logical organisation of the words not only helps us to understand them, but also to remember them. Obviously we understand – and remember – the words a lot more easily when they read:

"How many miles is it to the nearest railway station?"

Taking a sentence of ten words listed haphazardly, this test involves finding the original order. Here are the words:

more	*is*
the	*tyrant*
is	*whoever*
harsh	*law*
than	*a*

You have one minute to study this list of words and rearrange them in a logical order to make up a sentence. Write the words in the table opposite in the correct sentence order. Score two points for each correct answer.

YOUR ANSWERS

Words chosen to form a sentence	Score
1.	
2.	
3.	
4.	
5.	
6.	
7.	
8.	
9.	
10.	
Total (out of 20)	

Answers on page 72

Answer for evaluation

"Whoever is more harsh than the law is a tyrant."

Answer analysis

1. This sentence comes from Vauvenargues (1715-1747).

2. If you have written *"Whoever is a tyrant is more harsh than the law"*, you can regard this as also being correct. However, it is worth noting that although this sentence conveys the meaning of the original one and has a logical order, it is not as close to the normal style of language.

Remember

To communicate more easily:

• Organise the words logically in a sentence.

• Note that organisation helps comprehension.

COMPREHENSION CALLS FOR ORGANISATION

Disorganised writing defies comprehension because it is illogical. By reorganising it, you not only restore its sense and logic but you also develop your own reasoning power and a thought structure which helps you to memorise the text.

This test consists of of restoring the original construction of an extract from the novel *The Red and the Black* by Stendhal (1783-1842).

To restore a logical pattern, you first need to carefully read all the sentences, which make up a conversation between Julien Sorel and his father. Then, like a detective, you have to search for the clues, in particular those concerning time and place. Such clues reveal a logical link between the sentences.

You only have to reconstruct the dialogue. To help you, the last paragraph – K – of the extract is in its correct place at the very end of the extract. When you come to complete the test, mark your answers in the table on page 75, from 1 to 10, in the order you believe to be correct, using the corresponding letters before each sentence.

You have five minutes to study the sentences and put them in the right order. Score two points for each correct answer.

The text

A. *"But who will I eat with?"*

B. *"What will I get for that?"*

C. *"I have never spoken to her," Julien replied. " I have never seen this lady except in church."*

D. *"I don't want to be a servant."*

E. *"Answer me without lying, if you can, you lazy good-for-nothing; where do you know Madame de Rênal from, when have you spoken to her?"*

F. *"Yet there's something behind that," replied the cunning peasant, and he went quiet for a moment; "but I don't want anything to do with you, you deceitful wretch. In fact, I am going to be rid of you and my saw will work all the better for it. You won over the priest, who has found you a good place. Go and get packed and I'll take you to Monsieur de Rênal's house, where you are to be private tutor for the children."*

G. *"You swine, who is talking to you about being a servant? Do I want my son to be a servant?"*

H. *"But surely you would have seen her, you bare-faced liar?"*

I. *"Food, clothes and three hundred francs in wages."*

J. *"Never! You know that in church I have eyes only for God," added Julien, slightly hypocritically, quite properly in his view, to avoid being clouted again.*

K. *The question threw old Sorel, who felt that if he replied he would regret it; he lost his temper with Julien and showered him with insults, accusing him of greediness, and then went to consult his other sons.*

The text K is in the right place. You only need to rearrange the order of the dialogue before it.

YOUR ANSWERS

Corresponding letters in the correct order	Score
1.	
2.	
3.	
4.	
5.	
6.	
7.	
8.	
9.	
10.	
Total (out of 20)	

Answers on page 76

Answers for evaluation

1.	E		6.	B
2.	C		7.	I
3.	H		8.	D
4.	J		9.	G
5.	F		10.	A

Answer analysis

1. Here is the original text:

    "Answer me without lying, if you can, you lazy good-for-nothing; where do you know Madame de Rênal from, when have you spoken to her?"

    "I have never spoken to her," Julien replied. "I have never seen this lady except in church."

    "But surely you would have seen her, you bare-faced liar?"

    "Never! You know that in church I have eyes only for God,"added Julien slightly hypocritically, quite properly in his view, to avoid being clouted again.

    "Yet there's something behind that," replied the cunning peasant, and he went quiet for a moment; "but I don't want anything to do with you, you deceitful wretch. In fact, I am going to be rid of you and my saw will be all the better for it. You won over the priest, who has found you a good place. Go and get packed and I'll take you to Monsieur de Rênal's house, where you are to be private tutor for the children."

    "What will I get for that?"

    "Food, clothes and three hundred francs in wages."

    "I don't want to be a servant."

    "You swine, who is talking to you about being a servant? Do I want my son to be a servant?"

    "But who will I eat with?"

    This question threw old Sorel, who felt that if he replied he would regret it; he lost his temper with Julien and showered him with insults, accusing him of greediness, and then went to consult his other sons.

2. You know that it is a conversation between old Sorel and his son Julien. So the dialogue alternates between them.

3. You can be sure that last sentence of the conversation (10) must be a question from Julien which *"threw old Sorel"*. This question can only be sentence A because it is unexpected and preposterous.

4. If sentence 10 is a question from Julien, then you know by deduction that his father opens the dialogue and speaks all the odd-numbered sentences (1, 3, 5, 7 and 9).

5. Sentence 1 can only be *"Answer me without lying..."*. In all the other sentences spoken by the father there are:
    - conjunctions or linking words (*but, yet*),
    - nouns (*servant*),
    - pronouns (*her* for *Madame de Rênal*),
    which refer to a name previously mentioned.

6. Once you have the first sentence, Julien's reply is clear since he uses similar words (*"I have never spoken to her"*).

7. Having established the first two sentences, the dialogue can be linked up quite easily, especially since words or phrases are repeated in the replies (*church, servant*).

Comment

Naturally, if you get the first sentence wrong it will throw out your entire list and you will score nothing for the test, even if the rest of your answers are in the correct order.

Remember

To reconstruct a text:
- Read it carefully right through.
- Make a note of the clues, links and repetitions.
- Identify the logical connections.

HUNT THE INTRUDERS

One word is out of place in each of the following five lists. Identify the 'intruder' and write it down.

In each list seven words have a logical link between them. The 'odd one out' is the word that, despite appearances, has no direct connection with the others.

You have two minutes to study the lists and find the five intruding words. Score two points for each correct answer.

List 1

gander

crow

duck

chicken

guinea-fowl

cock

turkey

goose

List 2

paprika

tarragon

clove

cumin

coriander

watercress

saffron

chervil

List 3

Walter Scott

Thomas Hardy

Charlotte Brontë

Rudyard Kipling

William Shakespeare

George Elliott

Graham Greene

Kingsley Amis

List 4

geranium

fuchsia

rhododendron

philodendron

cyclamen

hibiscus

begonia

rose

List 5

dictionary

encyclopaedia

directory

index

catalogue

lexicon

diary

register

YOUR ANSWERS

List	Intruding word	Score
1		
2		
3		
4		
5		
	Total (out of 10)	

Answers on page 80

Answers for evaluation

1. Crow
2. Watercress
3. William Shakespeare
4. Philodendron
5. Diary

Answer analysis

1. The lists cover different subjects, within each of which groupings there is a logical thread.

2. In **List 1**, all the creatures mentioned are birds. But the *crow,* unlike the others, is not part of a traditional farm-yard environment.

3. **List 2** is primarily made up of spices, which excludes *watercress.*

4. Finding the 'intruder' in **List 3** may seem a little more difficult, since all the names are of famous writers. However *William Shakespeare* gained his reputation as a playwright, while the others are all novelists. A slight catch here, since some may be tempted to put Charlotte Brontë down as the only woman. Wrong. George Elliott was also a woman.

5. In **List 4**, the *philodendron* is the only plant that does not flower.

6. The *diary* is the only one in **List 5** where the information is organised chronologically. In all the other cases it is presented in alphabetical or similar order.

Remember

To hunt the intruders:

• Identify the family.

- Note the word that does not fit in with the family and exclude it.

THE BRAIN AND ITS HEMISPHERES

The brain is without doubt a most complex organ. Moreover, it reveals its mysteries sparingly. The most significant discoveries as to how it functions have only been made in the last twenty years.

What does it look like?
The brain looks very much like a walnut. And, as with that nut, it is divided into two parts – the left and right hemispheres.

If you look at the contours of a walnut, you will see that they are made up of winding, irregular lines which resemble the convolutions of the brain. The two halves are identical in appearance and are linked by a base which seals them so well that you have to break the nut to separate them. In the same way the two hemispheres of the brain are joined together by numerous nerve fibres.

Different but complementary roles
For a long time scientists were persuaded that the two parts of the brain had strictly identical roles. What in reality does each do?

The motor functions
The two parts of the brain do effectively have the same functions. But, since there is a cross-over, the left hemisphere governs the right-hand side of the body and the right hemisphere the left.

Other functions
The two hemispheres share the work. The left one is notably the centre for speech, logical analysis and linear thought. The right handles intuition, emotion, associations and our artistic senses.

ORGANISING CLUES LOGICALLY

Here you are presented with two mysteries, the object being to train and develop the capabilities of the left hemisphere. You need to imagine that you are the police inspector or a detective charged with investigating each of the incidents.

What details are you going to note and use in your detection?

With the help of your powers of logic, you must resolve both mysteries. The first is easier than the second. However, both call for a logical approach.

Look carefully for the clues and organise them in order to reconstruct the actual events.

You have five minutes to resolve the first mystery, having familiarised yourself with all the facts. You might only need five minutes for the second, but as a precaution allow yourself 24 hours to find the solution!

This section – **Organising clues logically** – is not so much a test as a pleasantly amusing exercise to end the chapter on **Organisation**. There is, therefore, not an answer sheet.

Mystery One

A managing director, known for being honest and trustworthy, rings the police station.

"A man obviously up to no good has just forced his way into my office and threatened me. You know that my business involves valuable materials, which is why I keep a gun to hand. Faced with the obvious danger this individual presented, I took my revolver out of the desk drawer, aimed it at his heart, fired and killed him. I was acting in self-defence."

A few minutes later the police inspector arrived on the scene accompanied by two detectives. The dead man was known to the police, with whom he had already been in trouble. The body was stretched out on its back, facing the desk of the industrialist, who was a friend of the inspector. The dead man was large and wearing black trousers, a white shirt and a bulky grey jacket with a chequered pattern of darker grey stripes.

The industrialist explained:

"When he came into my office, his right hand was in the back pocket of his trousers. He told me to open the safe. It was at that moment that I grabbed my revolver. I only fired once. He fell dead on to the floor."

The victim had a blood-stained hole in his jacket. The inspector knelt down and took a gun out of the man's back trouser pocket. Then he turned towards the industrialist.

"There's no need to worry old chap. The affair is quite clear. It's a typical case of justified self-defence."

It was then that one of the two detectives leant over the dead body, unbuttoned the jacket and lifted the left-hand side of it, which he let drop immediately and said:

"I am sorry for your friend, Inspector, but he must be arrested because the man stretched out on the floor has been murdered."

What did the detective notice in order to arrive at this conclusion?

YOUR ANSWER

Do not look at the paragraph on the next page headed 'Answer' before replying. You have five minutes, having studied the facts contained in the enigma.

Write your answer here:

....

....

....

....

Answer

At a glance the detective noticed that the impact of the bullet in the jacket did not correspond with that in the shirt. It was lower. In other words the intruder, who was supposed to have been threatening the industrialist, must have had his hands in the air when he received the bullet right in the middle of his heart. And this, of course, puts paid to the idea of self-defence.

Answer analysis

Here organisation, structured thinking and logic helped prevent a miscarriage of justice. Everything had appeared, however, to point to the fact that the well-respected industrialist was in the right.

Similar cases to this one happen every day, according to the records.

A logical progression, based on concrete facts, is often more valuable than a subjective judgement, *a fortiori* when you find yourself in a situation which on the surface seems cut-and-dried.

Mystery Two

The incident takes place one Friday evening in an isolated inn on the edge of a wood. Mr and Mrs Brown go inside. The old clock strikes eight. The large dining room on the ground floor is empty except for the landlord, who is standing behind the bar. He is awaiting his guests for the weekend. A brief conversation ensues:

"I am Mr Brown. I have booked a room for two."

"Fine. Here is the key. You are in Number Three on the first floor."

The Browns go upstairs, then come back down a few minutes later and settle themselves in one corner of the large deserted dining room.

A quarter of an hour later, another couple arrives. The Smiths are also expected for the weekend. The landlord gives them the key to Number Four. They also take their bags up to their room, then return and, giving the Browns a polite nod of the head, go to sit at the far end of the dining room and order their meal.

At this stage of the story, it is important to note that the Browns and the Smiths do not know each other, have never seen each other before and have nothing in common and equally nothing to fear from each other.

When the meal is finished, Mr Brown remarks casually to Mr Smith, who is smiling at him:
"At least it's quiet here."
Then he adds:
"Perhaps you would like to join us for coffee."
For a while the Browns and the Smiths sit together at the same table, chatting away in a friendly fashion. However, the two women are tired and go up to their respective bedrooms while the husbands light up cigars and order drinks.

Here follows a scenario between the two men which you have to reconstruct to resolve the puzzle.

Suddenly Mr Smith gets up, walks across to the stairs and starts going up to his room. At this moment, Mr Brown also gets up, pulls a gun out of his pocket, fires at Mr Smith's legs and then falls down dead.

What happened?

YOUR ANSWER

Do not even glance at the answer on page 87 before replying.

You have up to 24 hours – that's the maximum – to resolve this mystery.

Write your answer here:

....

....

....

....

....

....

....

....

....

....

....

....

....

....

....

....

Answer

- Mr Brown and Mr Smith were having a good chat and had started talking about what they did for a living and what interests they had.

- Mr Smith's profession has absolutely no significance as far as this puzzle is concerned.

- Mr Brown's profession gives him the right to carry a firearm. He could, for example, be a policeman.

- Mr Brown claims to have the gift of hypnosis.

- Mr Smith replies that he does not believe at all in things like that, that he has a very down-to-earth mind and only believes what he sees.

- Mr Brown proposes carrying out an experiment to show him.

- Mr Smith accepts because he is convinced that Mr Brown will not be able to hypnotise him.

- Then Mr Brown gives him the following order: "Go up to your room and strangle your wife." But he says to himself that when Mr Smith has his hands on his wife's neck he will wake him up and be able to claim triumphantly: "So, my friend, you still don't believe in hypnosis?"

- Mr Smith, who is under hypnosis, starts to go upstairs to carry out the order Mr Brown has given him.

- But Mr Brown suddenly has heart trouble. He realises his heart is giving up and he will not be able to 'wake' Mr Smith. He wants at all costs to stop him committing the irrevocable. So, with Mr Smith already at the foot of the stairs, he has no other choice but to shoot him in the legs to wake him up and prevent him from strangling his wife. Then he collapses, victim of a heart attack.

Answer analysis

1. This mystery carries a certain number of clues which need to be arranged with patience and logic.

2. Two men who do not know each other and who speak together in a friendly and calm way almost always get round to the subject of work, what each does for a living and what their interests are.

3. Naturally, Mr Brown may prefer to talk about his talent as a hypnotist, rather than discuss his everyday job.

4. It is clearly stated that Mr Brown fires at Mr Smith's legs, so there is no intention to kill him, but rather to give him a message, since immediately Mr Brown falls down dead.

5. The fact that he dies so suddenly can obviously be put down to a heart attack.

PRACTICAL CONSEQUENCES

You can regard parts of this chapter as recreation. However, it is completely centred round the idea that it is easier to remember what is organised. So if you have, for example, a lesson to learn, the best way is to extract the essentials using a very visual structure. Then it is just a matter of keeping this scheme in your memory, since the rest of the information will hang easily round it.

Imagine, for example, a lesson on colonial expansion. You can distribute the information on three pages, referring to the three main themes of interest: 1. CAUSES; 2. FACTS; 3. CONSEQUENCES.

Below is an example of how to visualise CAUSES, using a tree structure, which will enable you to keep all the relevant facts in your memory. You can work out for yourself how to tackle FACTS and CONSEQUENCES using the same method.

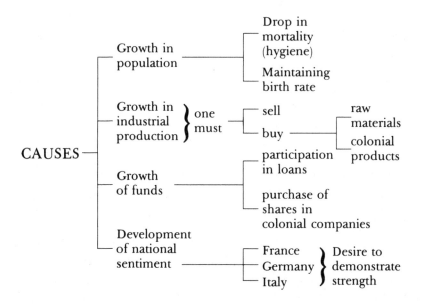

CHAPTER III

OBSERVE

in order to memorise

We see, but we do not always notice.

Every day a whole cascade of images passes in front of our eyes. How many are caught in the net of our sight? Very few. Why? Because we have not taken the time to observe them. However – and it is the same in all fields – time does not like us to ignore it.

We regularly take the same route but are still not able to describe it in any great detail. More often than not the changes that take place around us escape our sense of observation. They pass unnoticed even though we have seen them.

Can you, for example, describe the decor in your local bakery shop? How many times have you 'discovered' or 'seen' for the first time a trinket, a painting or whatever object that has been sitting there under your very eyes for months? Have you never asked a friend if he has just repainted his living room when he has done nothing to it, even though you frequently call in? Until this particular day you have never really opened your eyes to notice the colour of the walls.

- Observing is allowing your look to take its time, to notice details and to go in search of precision.

- Observing is getting your sight to contribute to a re-discovery of the world that makes up your environment. Life in the fast lane, stress, the habit of always going that bit quicker, all constitute barriers to observation, and lead us to neglect an important mass of information which becomes permanently buried in the unconscious, in the store of images that are never revived.

- Observing is a little like learning how to live again, rediscovering the shapes, colours and objects that make up our universe.

- Observing is exchanging a passive gaze, which is quite enough for the average television viewer, for an active gaze, which is not content with just seeing.

- Observing is developing our memory.

In this chapter, different tests highlight the value of observation and the role it plays in our memory. In particular they involve the capacity to retain information accepted into the visual memory.

Through these tests, which have deliberately not always been quantified, you will develop in particular your power of observation and your visual memory.

DISCOVERING THE FAMILIAR WORLD

We tend in some way to lose contact with objects that are all around us. Without going as far as forgetting them, we very often have an image of them that is more blurred than we imagine.

This test is aimed at making you rediscover the world around you. You have two minutes to answer the questions.

Bearing in mind the purely subjective nature of this first task, there is no scoring.

1. A room in the house

You go into your kitchen every day, but are you able to recall its details precisely?

- Describe the way in which it is laid out.

- Describe the objects which are in it, in the order in which they are arranged.

2. Books

Are you able to locate a particular book on the correct shelf without any hesitation? Reply immediately to the following questions:

- Where is the dictionary?

- Describe its cover without looking at it.

- Roughly how many books do you have?

3. Music

You almost certainly have a collection of records, compact discs or cassettes. Select a title at random.

- Describe, without looking at it, the illustration that appears on the cover or front of the packaging.

- Detail the following:
  - the colours
  - the shape of the lettering
  - the design of the picture.

4. The car

When you reply to the following three questions, take the car that you use or are driven in most often.

- Describe precisely the dashboard of the car.

- How many sign symbols are there?

- Specify them.

5. At work

If you work in a business:

- Try to make a plan of the site or building.

- How many offices are there?

- What colour are the doors?

- What colour are the walls?

If you are a student or pupil, answer the same questions but substitute class rooms for offices.

6. Photos and illustrations

Picture in your mind a photo that you have – preferably one in which there are several people. Then take a piece of paper and describe on it what is represented in the photo, trying not to leave out any detail.

a) The people

- Begin by writing down the number of people in the photo.

- Spend time detailing what each is wearing.

- Describe their relative positions (who is sitting down, who is standing up, etc).
- Describe their faces:
  - expression
  - hairstyle
  - glasses (if any)
- What are they wearing on their heads:
  - scarf?
  - hat?

b) *The background*

- Is it outside? In which case, describe the natural surroundings (garden, beach, mountain, etc).
- Is it indoors? In which case, detail:
  - the furniture
  - the decor (wallpaper, carpet, chair covers, etc)
  - the objects in the room

Repeat this exercise using an illustration or an image from a piece of publicity, for example.

Always remember to check what you have said against the original photo afterwards. This will enable you to measure accurately your power of observation.

Compare . . .

Each time you do a test like this, verify it afterwards by comparing what you have written down on your piece of paper with the reality. Check it against the original photo, illustration or advertisement.

. . . and note

- Everything you have forgotten.
- All the details that have escaped your visual memory.
- Be as accurate as possible in order to make progress. Above all, do not cheat. This way you will develop your powers of observation at the same time as your memory.

ON THE DOORSTEP

There would appear to be nothing easier than memorising a stylised house. Nevertheless, one is aware that it is not enough just to *see* in order to reconstitute the information as accurately as possible. Again, it is necessary to *look* and *register* in order to put one's faculties of observation to work. Sometimes one has to make an extra effort to ensure certain images are planted in one's brain.

There is absolutely no trap in this test. First, you have to look at the drawing of the house below for 15 seconds. Then go through the questions that follow and the advice given about this test, without looking again at the drawing.

Questions

- How many windows did you see?

- How many shutters have hearts?

- How many windows have curtains?

- How many rows of tiles are there on the roof?

- How many window-panes have you spotted?

- How many rows of bricks are there on the chimney?

- How many windows are there on the first floor?

- How many windows have shutters?

- How many different motifs decorate the shutters?

- How many rounded shapes have you noticed?

Read through these questions very carefully. You will find them abbreviated in the table opposite. Beside each of the questions, write the number you think is correct.

You have two minutes to answer the questions. Score two points for each correct answer.

WE HAVE SAID 'OBSERVE'

To observe, from the Latin *observare*, means to make one's behaviour conform with that prescribed by the law, but also to consider with application or examine, regard in an attentive way, notice ... So, if to observe is to regard with attention, to regard with attention is to start to understand. And to start to understand is to learn to reformulate, which is to train oneself to remember. One can therefore say that to observe is to practise a language for laying down the foundations for a certain form of memory.

YOUR ANSWERS

	Answer	Score
1. *Number of windows*		
2. *Number of shutters with hearts*		
3. *Number of windows with curtains*		
4. *Number of rows of tiles*		
5. *Number of window panes*		
6. *Number of rows of chimney bricks*		
7. *Number of first-floor windows*		
8. *Number of windows with shutters*		
9. *Number of different motifs on the shutters*		
10. *Number of rounded shapes*		
Total (out of 20)		

Answers on page 98

Answers for evaluation

1	–	4	6 – 3	
2	–	2	7 – 3	
3	–	1	8 – 3	
4	–	4	9 – 3	
5	–	14	10 – 8	

Answer analysis

1. One is conscious, even having been warned, of the difficulty of memorising what one thought one had looked at.

2. Different strategies were possible. On the one hand, a photographic image of the whole which could be reconstituted by our visual memory. On the other hand, rigorous and systematic observation of all the elements contained in this very schematic house, using some logical and progressive principle of one's choice. *Example:* one could start by the front door and move on to look at the ground-floor window (panes, shutters and motifs), then spend time observing all the elements of the first floor, before finishing with the roof and chimney.

3. In **Question 10**, the central window on the first floor includes two rounded shapes and not four, since one must take into account the whole of each curtain.

Remember

To memorise what you have observed:

• Work towards a photographic image of the whole.

• Work towards a systematic observation of all of the elements, following a logical progression.

TIME FOR OBSERVATION

This is not a test in the proper sense of the word. You are being asked to look at the drawing below for 15 seconds and then redraw it in the boxed area provided. For this exercise, you have one minute.

It is not your talent as an artist that matters here, but rather your ability to remember what you have seen.

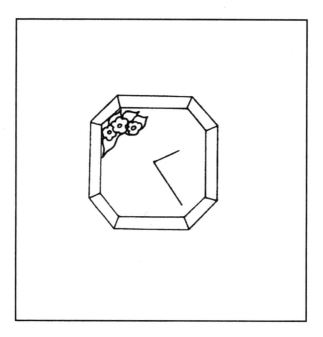

YOUR DRAWING

Verification

1. Compare your drawing with the original.

2. Go through what you left out, what you got wrong and what you added and make a note of them here:

....

....

....

....

....

....

THE WAITERS' MEMORY

Some waiters never remember who ordered what. Others, on the other hand, deserve our admiration. They are capable of remembering several different orders, not only from a single table but also throughout the restaurant. They never serve a coffee to someone who asked for a lemonade.

What is their secret? How can one explain their prodigious memory. In fact there are several possible ways in which to achieve the same result.

Some work particularly by association. They take orders to a system and, by observation, associate them immediately with the right customer without confusing which customer asked for what.

Others, using a kind of permanent mental gymnastics, remember particularly well because they concentrate and put all their attention on their work.

Then there are those who simply enjoy the job and whose motivation strengthens the memory.

None of these methods conflict and often they combine in the same waiter. However, in the majority of waiters, just one of these characteristics dominates even though the others may also be present.

MATCHING THE IMAGES

This test relies essentially on the visual memory. Opposite is a panel with ten boxes. Inside each box there is an image. These boxes have deliberately not been numbered, in order to avoid involving the associative memory. It is therefore simply a matter of retaining what the retina has placed in your brain.

The Ancient Greeks and Romans attached quite a special importance to images. They held the view that sight was superior to the other senses, which is why they used it for memorising their speeches, notably with the method of *loci*, which we have already discussed at the beginning of the book.

Remember that it is impossible to memorises places and images without observation.

You have one minute to look at these ten pictures. Then turn over the page to the answer form and write in each of the empty spaces the name of the image that relates to that box, without any further reference to the ten illustrations.

Score two points for each correct answer, making a maximum of four points for each correct line.

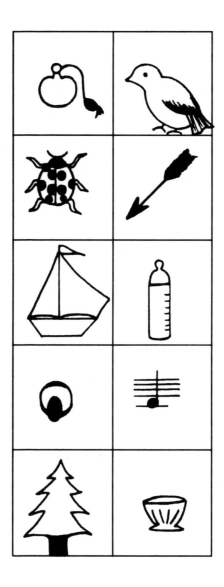

YOUR ANSWERS

Name of picture in each box in correct order		Score
	Total (out of 20)	

WHAT DO WE REMEMBER BEST AND WHEN?

- We remember best what we like.
- We remember best what interests us.
- We remember best if there is emotion (a strong sensation of intense pleasure or deep pain – all emotional shocks leave their mark on the brain).
- We remember best if we are motivated.
- We remember best when we pay attention.
- We remember best when we have understood properly.
- We remember best when we concentrate.
- We remember best what we put in order in our memory.

Answer analysis

1. You will obviously have compared your answers with the original panel of pictures in order to mark up your score. Perhaps you will have noticed some mistakes or omissions. Perhaps you will have answered correctly throughout.

2. To memorise this type of picture panel correctly, it is not a question of working on type associations (such as animals – bird and ladybird – for example). On the contrary, you have to rely on your sight, which must print in the brain not only the picture but at the same time its position.

Remember

To have a faithful visual memory:

- *Observe* and do not be content just to *see* what you must retain.

- Assimilate the image and the place simultaneously.

- Reply quickly, since this type of exercise relies on the immediate memory.

OBSERVATION MUST NOT DECEIVE

This is not so much a test as an exercise in observation – and more difficult than the previous one. There are eight more pictures to memorise. The object is to remember them in the order in which they are presented.

You have one minute to look at the drawings. Then, using the spaces in the table on page 108, write in the name of each object in its correct order.

THE DANGER OF MAKING ASSERTIONS

The inaccurate reporting of a fact, supposedly accurately observed, has often been the source of conflict, of misunderstanding or, even more serious, of unintentionally supplying false evidence, in all good faith.

To make an assertion about something one has been able to observe always presents an element of risk. Exercises of the kind we are giving you in this book, which do not put anyone's destiny in danger, demonstrate quite clearly the fragility of the visual memory while, at the same time, helping to develop it.

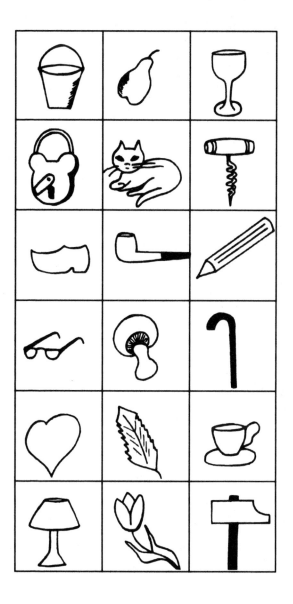

YOUR ANSWERS

Write the names of all the images in the panel you have just looked at in the corresponding spaces in the table below.

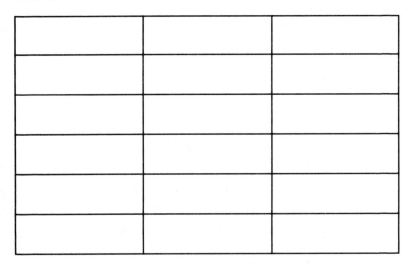

Answers on page 110

Remember

To observe without risking any mistakes:

• Memorise each picture and its position simultaneously.

• Do not assume too quickly that what you think you recall really is the case.

OBSERVATION AND MEMORY

In current language, 'to make an observation' to someone means 'to make a remark' – that is to say, 'to mark again'. This expression is not without significance, since to know how to observe implies that one knows how to remember and also recall.

Observation occurs because we want to 'mark' a fact, an expression or whatever, in our mind, firmly and permanently. But the very certainty of a precise observation runs the risk of leading to a distorted recollection which does not tally with the reality. It is the open door to unintentional false evidence, to misunderstandings, and to confusion.

So, one must learn to 'lock in' one's observation in order to check the original information already fixed in one's brain. For that, one simply has to shut one's eyes for a few seconds, empty one's mind and then look again to make sure that the original image and the checked image are identical. Under these conditions, observation supplies the memory with reliable material.

Answers

Bucket	Pear	Glass
Padlock	Cat	Corkscrew
Clog	Pipe	Pencil
Glasses	Mushroom	Walking stick
Heart	Leaf	Cup
Lamp	Flower	Hammer

Answer analysis

1. There is no scoring in this exercise. It is simply intended to reinforce the previous test, which you have already marked.

2. Out of the 18 pictures you had to memorise and place in their correct boxes:

    - If you have less than ten correct answers, you need to work on your visual memory.

    - If you have 10-13 correct answers, your visual memory is satisfactory, but you must work at developing it.

    - If you have 14-16 correct answers, your visual memory is very good, but you should still exercise it so that it is even better.

    - If you have 17-18 correct answers, congratulations! You have an excellent visual memory. Look after it!

A MEMORY FOR NUMBERS

To develop your power of observation, you need to exercise it on different things.

The panel below contains ten boxes, inside each of which there is a different number. Although the numbers can be considered like the pictures, you do not in fact use the same method for memorising them. If you look at 37 and 26, for example, you could quite easily reproduce them incorrectly as 27 and 36. On the other hand, you could not muddle up a cat with a ladle or a flute with a broom.

To achieve a good score in this test, you are advised not to try and find any meanings or associations but to absorb the numbers in their entirety with a good, hard look. This is the key to observation. You do not have sufficient time to find a mnemonic method and store the information in a drawer of your long-term or even medium-term memory.

You have only one minute to look at the numbers, before reproducing them – in their correct positions – in the empty boxes of the answer panel that follows.

Score two points for each correct answer, making a maximum score of four points for each correct row.

32	11
4	28
25	9
18	14
17	58

YOUR ANSWERS

Numbers in correct order		Score
	Total (out of 20)	

For answers refer to grid on page 111.

Answer analysis

1. Numbers are more difficult to remember than objects because we do not think of them as images.

2. If, in your daily life, you want to develop this sense of observation, practise remembering, for example, the prices of articles displayed in a shop-window (and not just those that interest you) or the local bus timetable (if it is not too long!).

Remember

To retain a panel of numbers through observation:

*   Think of them as images.
*   Absorb them as an entirety.

WHEN GEOMETRY PLAYS ITS PART

This drawing is a geometric abstract. Look at it for one minute, cover it up, and then reproduce it in the empty space opposite. This is an exercise and not a test.

YOUR ANSWER

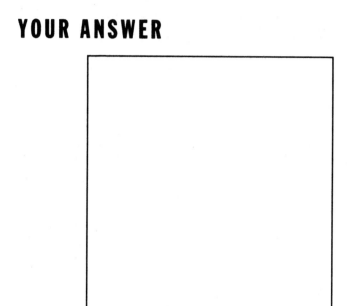

Compare your drawing with the original.

Answer analysis

1. An abstract design is a lot more difficult to remember than a realistic drawing, especially when it is very detailed.

2. Do not worry about your ability as a draughtsman. The point of this exercise is to evaluate your ability to remember shapes and their position in a given area.

Remember

To memorise an abstract geometric design:

- Force yourself to take a fresh look when observing an unusual geometric drawing which has no reference in your traditional cultural code.

- A fresh look presupposes a memory that is ready to accept non-stereotypical information.

A CLUSTER OF STARS

This test relies on your ability to remember the position of figures in a given space. The panel opposite contains ten boxes. Inside each there are four stars. You have to reproduce the exact position of these stars in their corresponding boxes in the answer panel that follows.

There is no point of reference in any of the boxes. So you have to 'photograph' the different positions of the stars contained in the boxes before completing this test.

Imagine what a map of the night sky could offer! Here, at least the stars are not revolving. They are fixed inside each box.

You have one minute to look at the ten boxes. Score two points for every perfectly correct answer (approximations do not count). The maximum score for each row of correct answers is four points.

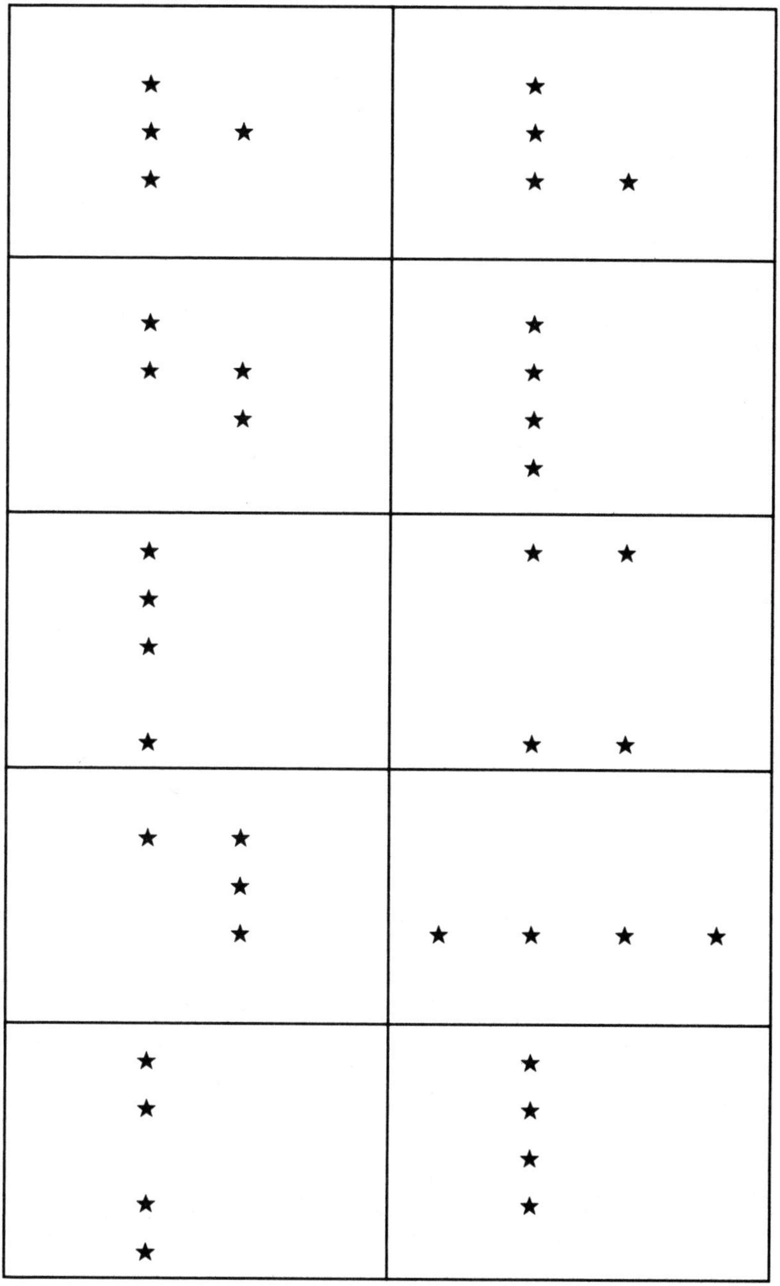

YOUR ANSWERS

Position of stars		Score
	Total (out of 20)	

Compare your positions with the original panel.

Answer analysis

1. Approximations have been dismissed as unacceptable since they reveal a flaw in your method of memorising the positions of elements in a given space.

2. The systematic positioning of four elements in identical square spaces makes visual memory easier.

3. What you needed to register was the sideways movement of the stars' positions.

Remember

To help the visual memory with changing positions in open spaces:

- Photograph the position of the elements.

- Note the type of position change they undergo.

GEOMETRIC SYMPHONY

This exercise presents a few difficulties.

The panel you have to look at contains 18 geometric designs, each of which occupies a specific place. If it was a panel of traffic signals, for example, this visual memory exercise would offer no particular problem because it would represent symbols that were coded, universally known and familiar.

Here there is no logic behind the collection of designs which have absolutely nothing in common with each other. So your memory has to rely solely on observation to reproduce the contents of the panel in the correct order.

The aim of this exercise is to develop your visual memory.

Having looked at the designs for two minutes, you have to reproduce them in the corresponding empty boxes in the answer panel that follows.

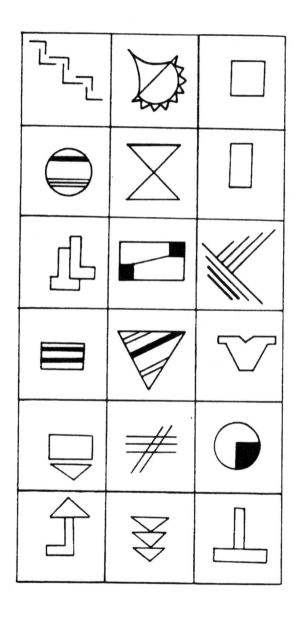

Compare your drawings with the original panel.

Answer analysis

1. This exercise reinforces the one entitled '**When geometry plays its part**'. However, the number of designs to remember is increased from one to 18. Each design required very special observation.

2. The difficulty with this exercise rests in memorising shapes, most of which have no reference in our cultural code. On the whole, they do not resemble any object in everyday life. This is therefore a purely visual exercise which requires one's immediate memory to store numerous elements and details, rather than a coherent design.

Remember

To memorise geometric designs:

* Do not neglect to observe details.
* Develop a memory for shapes.

KIM'S GAME

This is a very well-known game.

You have a panel containing 35 drawings. You are not going to be asked to write down the names of all the objects you have seen in the equivalent blank panel and still less to reproduce them! However, the questions you have to answer will certainly not be what you are expecting.

Look at the panel for two minutes. You will then have to answer 20 questions. Some of them simply require a *yes* or *no*, while others will need a number.

Score one point for each correct answer.

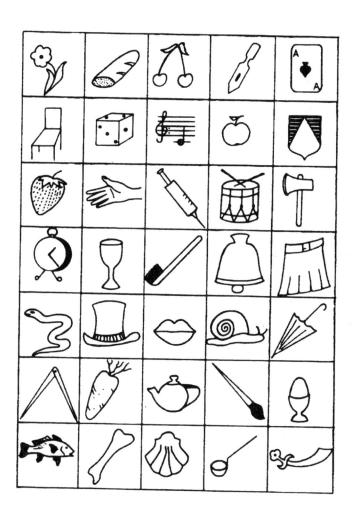

YOUR ANSWERS

Kim's game	Answer	Score
1. *Number of animals*		
2. *The fingers of the hand are spread apart*		
3. *There are three different fruits*		
4. *Number of visible dots on the dice*		
5. *Number of items of furniture*		
6. *The shield is above the playing card*		
7. *The playing card is the ace of clubs*		
8. *Number of flowers*		
9. *Number of cutting objects*		
10. *The alarm clock reads 1.25*		
11. *The bread has been cut*		
12. *Number of musical instruments*		
13. *There is nothing edible in the middle column*		
14. *There are two vegetables*		
15. *The teapot has a lid*		
16. *Number of horizontal rows*		
17. *Number of leaves on the apple stalk*		
18. *The skirt has a design on it*		
19. *The lips are closed*		
20. *There is only one paint-brush*		
Total (out of 20)		

Answers on page 128

THE ORIGIN OF KIM'S GAME

What we know as 'Kim's Game' comes from the novel Kim (1901) written by Rudyard Kipling. Kim O'Hara, orphan of an Irish sergeant in the Indian Army, is a child of Lahore, capital of Tendjad. He becomes a pupil of a Tibetan lama, whom he follows across India. He carries important messages for the British secret service and eventually one Colonel Creighton decides to make him a secret agent.

Kim undergoes intensive training with the aim of developing his memory. In no time at all he is capable of naming 20 precious stones that are shown to him, as well as giving all their different peculiarities.

It was by practising a similar exercise, but looking quickly at objects placed in a shop-window and trying afterwards to describe them in detail, that the great conjurer Robert Houdin acquired his prestigious memory.

Kim's Game, which has a number of variations, is played by adults and children alike and is also used in psychology. Different objects are placed on the ground or on a table. The players look at them for a few moments, after which the objects are removed and everyone has to make a list of what was there.

Comment

When one is looking instead of seeing, one very often does not know what it will be useful to observe. Those who have used their visual memory for this test, will perhaps have remembered the majority of the drawings in the panel and their positions. But they were not able to guess the nature of the questions that were going to be asked.

For this reason, one must observe in an open minded way, that is to say from a wide angle, and not for the purpose of a presupposed answer to an anticipated question.

Answers for evaluation

1.	3		11.	Yes
2.	Yes		12.	1
3.	Yes		13.	No
4.	6		14.	No
5.	1		15.	Yes
6.	No		16.	7
7.	No		17.	1
8.	1		18.	No
9.	2		19.	Yes
10.	Yes		20.	Yes

Answer analysis

1. 3 animals: snake, fish and snail.

2. Yes, the fingers of the hand are spread apart.

3. Yes, strawberry, apple and cherry (there are two but they count as one fruit).

4. 6 dots visible on the dice.

5. A chair.

6. No, the shield is under the playing-card.

7. No, the card is the ace of spades.

8. 1 flower.

9. 2 cutting objects: axe and sabre.

10. Yes, the alarm-clock reads 1.25.

11. Yes, the bread has been cut.

12. 1 musical instrument: drum

13. No. There is something edible because the cherries figure in the middle vertical column.

14. No. There is only one: a carrot.

15. Yes, the teapot has its lid on.

16. There are 7 horizontal rows.

17. There is 1 leaf on the apple stalk.

18. No, the skirt does not have a design on it.

19. Yes, the lips are closed.

20. Yes, there is only one paint-brush.

Remember

To observe a series of different elements one after the other:

• Practise three types of observation at a time:

The *accountant's regard* for scanning and registering all the numerical information, all the quantifiable data, for fixing the management of space and the organisation of the elements well in his memory.

The *painter's regard* for photographing the shapes, the graphic relationships, the harmony or the anachronisms, for seeing certain elements bordering on or overlapping with others.

The *detective's regard* for observing the anomalies, things that are bizarre, but also the tiniest details.

Exercise

Practise Kim's Game with a variety of objects and set up a competition among a group of people. The comparison between the different results will clearly indicate the differences between the various types of memory.

CHAPTER IV

IMMEDIATE
Memory

Immediate memory is the basis of all memorising procedures. It allows us instant recall of information received. In this respect it is rather like an echo. Thanks to it, we can coherently control our movements, our speech and our thoughts. It represents the first stone of the edifice that is our long-term memory.

Immediate memory cannot cope with interference or diversions. Let us take an example. You look for a number in the telephone directory. You memorise it. But between the moment you shut the directory and when you go to dial the number, the door-bell rings. You open the door. Your immediate memory has been interfered with and you no longer remember the number. There has been a diversion that has nothing to do with your current mental activity.

We use our immediate memory every day and all the time. Its mechanism works all on its own, normally without our knowing it. It belongs to our mental breathing, our automatic activities, and without it nothing we undertake is possible. In effect, immediate memory represents a succession of short-distance relays; it enables us to ensure the continuity of our undertakings, to pursue what we have embarked upon and to establish a coherent sequence to a speech, an idea or whatever procedure we are engaged in.

Immediate memory is, in a kind of way, the absolutely indispensable fuel which provides us with access to all other memory forms.

The object of the following tests is to train our immediate memory for instant recall.

A CAREFUL SCAN

You have 40 seconds to run your eye over the three columns of words that follow. Then go straightaway to the question below to test your immediate memory.

wine	fatigue	wheel
for	salad	alarm-clock
moon	thief	blouse
region	raisin	return
artisan	signature	friendly
question	restaurant	resource
election	telephone	knowledge
use	reproach	reasonable
republican	information	traveller
affectionately	adventurer	courageous
educational	suspect	gymnastics
bus	major	passionate
radiator	library	news
multiplication	accident	perfection
police	power	elegance
clothes	reflection	grapefruit
historical	evidence	resistance
cinema	electricity	possibility
navigation	prairie	bungalow
refrigerator	painful	notice

Tick YES or NO depending on whether you think that the following words appear in the three columns you have just read. Of course, you must not refer back to the lists of words.

You have 30 seconds to give your 10 answers. Score two points for each correct answer.

YOUR ANSWERS

	YES	NO	Score
1. *news*			
2. *traveller*			
3. *prairie*			
4. *reproach*			
5. *election*			
6. *blouse*			
7. *telephone*			
8. *library*			
9. *multiplication*			
10. *artisan*			
Total (out of 20)			

Answers on page 136

MUSTER YOUR SENSES TO HELP YOUR MEMORY

In order to activate, look after and develop your memory, you must have all your senses permanently on. All the indicators must be working. The first 'memory' lesson you must teach yourself is always to be aware of the potential of your senses and learn to rediscover them. The memory requires the permanent contribution of all your sensory apparatus, notably:

- the visual (sight) memory

- the auditory (hearing) memory

- the olfactory (smell) memory

- the gustatory (taste) memory

- the tactile (touch) memory

In training yourself to develop one sense in particular, you inevitably develop a type of memory you can hook on to.

In this list, let us not forget the *motor memory*, the one that reacts mechanically because it has been acquired through habit. Thus certain people will retain a piece of text that they have written down themselves better than one which is printed. The movements fix themselves in the memory.

Then, on the fringe, there is the *emotional memory*, which certainly functions under the effect of intense fear. This memory is accidental, fortuitous, unforeseeable and no exercise will improve it.

Answers for evaluation

1.	news	=	yes		6.	blouse	=	yes
2.	traveller	=	yes		7.	telephone	=	yes
3.	prairie	=	yes		8.	library	=	yes
4.	reproach	=	yes		9.	multiplication	=	yes
5.	election	=	yes		10.	artisan	=	yes

Answer analysis

1. If you have 20 points, your immediate memory is excellent. Continue to look after it. If you have 16 or 18 points, your immediate memory is very good, but you need to test it out as often as possible. If you have 12 or 14 points, your immediate memory is good, but you could make rapid progress with some practice. If you have less than 12 points, it is essential that you work at developing your immediate memory. Rest assured, there is nothing easier!

2. To do this test, you called on your visual memory, the one you use for observing. But did you put your auditory memory to work? If you had read out loud, or simply to yourself, all the words that appeared in the three columns, you would probably have had better results.

Remember

To develop your immediate memory:

- Train your visual and auditory memories.
- Work on your sense of observation.
- Avoid interference.

IN THE WORD GARDEN

This test consists of reading the words written in the box below and then writing down all the ones you have remembered in the answer panel that follows.

You have 20 seconds for 'registering' the words. Score two points for each correct answer.

```
P
L
MORNING        BEE              RIVER
U
G
H                     START

                            BARGE

        SNOW

            POLLEN

    SPORT                    MAT
```

YOUR ANSWERS

Words remembered	Score
1.	
2.	
3.	
4.	
5.	
6.	
7.	
8.	
9.	
10.	
Total (out of 20)	

Answers on page 140

A THREE-DRAWER CHEST

Imagine a chest of drawers. In the first drawer there is the immediate memory. It has not got time to devote itself to a comprehensive acquisition of data for storage. It manages the immediate past and its field of activity does not stretch over more than about 15 seconds, except if an emotional shock occurs at the moment when its attention is alerted.

In the second drawer is the medium-term memory. It is involved in acquiring data in the way that will most encourage stock-piling and enable it to recall information quickly and easily several days later. It homes in on those things that we find interesting.

In the third drawer is the long-term memory. It is complex and vast, and never reveals its exact scope. You cannot see its limits. To enter the long-term memory the data has already passed through the sieve of the other two memories. This drawer holds the definitive store of collected memories – whether conscious or subconscious – some of which we believed were forgotten. This memory holds many elements of knowledge, of recollection and of the story of our life and is in direct contact with our feelings and emotions. The result of intentional training, it is also able to recall 'accidental' memories. And this accidental memory is most active in the field of emotions.

Answers for evaluation

1. morning
2. plough
3. sport
4. bee
5. start
6. snow
7. pollen
8. river
9. barge
10. mat

Answer analysis

1. There was no particular order that your answers needed to follow.

2. It was possible to establish some associations between different words:
   - sport/mat
   - barge/river
   - start/morning
   - snow/plough
   - bee/pollen

Remember

The immediate memory does not retain what it has taken in for more than half a minute and cannot grasp an item of information that lasts more than seven seconds.

THE NUMBERS GAME

You must exercise your immediate memory all the time on words, sentences and numbers as well as on situations, places, people, animals and images that pass before you.

Here is a panel containing nine numbers. You have ten seconds to look at it. Then turn over and write the numbers down in their correct boxes in the answer panel on the next page.

There is no scoring in this test.

9	4	7
1	6	3
5	2	8

YOUR ANSWERS

Answer analysis

1. Compare your answers with the original panel.

2. In a few seconds you could see that 1, 2, 3 and 4 formed a diamond, starting in the west, then going to the south and the east and finishing in the north. 5, 6 and 7 formed a diagonal from the south-west to the north-east. From the 8 in the south-east, one jump over the centre led to the 9 in the north-west.

3. You could have arrived at the same result relying entirely on your visual memory, by 'photographing' the panel of numbers.

4. A further method would be to remember the numbers in groups of three, following an order of your choice: 947 –163 – 528 or 915 – 462 – 738. Obviously it is easier to remember three groups of three numbers than nine separate numbers.

Remember

To restore what is scattered:

- Be aware that your immediate memory has the ability to recall instantly – the capacity to restore information immediately.

- The immediate memory has its limitations. For this reason, you must reproduce what has been temporarily registered at once, avoiding any disturbance which would interpose between the entry and recall of the data.

- If you have to commit numbers and letters to your immediate memory, remember that both respond to the law of grouping. Sometimes it is sufficient just to change the order of the letters, for example, in order to give them some significance. Thus, compare D.A.I.E.L. with I.D.E.A.L., which you can pronounce *'ideal'*.

CHAPTER V

MAKING LINKS
To Build Bridges

To associate is to establish links or relationships between a new element and one already known and stored in the memory.

Association is not something artificial, a procedure brought to the memory from outside or a method you have been unaware of for resurrecting memories. We all use it spontaneously in everyday life and very often without even thinking about it.

Imagine a friend telling you about his last holidays. What he says reminds you of experiences of your own and you interrupt him by saying: "That makes me think of . . ." or "That's just like me last year . . ." You have experienced an association of ideas. Your friend's story has prompted in your mind an association which you would undoubtedly not have talked about that evening had the conversation been about something different.

An unimportant detail, an advertising slogan or even a scrap of conversation overhead in the street can immediately send you off down memory lane.

145

As soon as a new piece of information reaches us, it finds an echo and links up with other information stored in our memory. This proves that:

- our memory stockpiles a large amount of information and
- one of the best ways of memorising involves playing with associations.

Association is divided into several types. Among the chief ones, there is:

1. **Indirect association:**

   A photo of a boat can make you think of a seafaring grandfather, which leads you to recall the image of your grandmother and then your holidays spent with them.

2. **Association by train of thought:**

   A match reminds one of fire, holidays of the sun, skiing of the mountains . . .

3. **Word association:**

   There are four types:
   - By root: free, freely, freedom.
   - By sense: synonyms come into this category – boat, ship, vessel.
   - By assonance: saw, soar, sore.
   - By resemblance: paronyms come into this category – eminent, imminent; affluence, influence.

4. **Association by opposites:**

   White/black

   Day/night

   Happiness/sadness

5. **Association by characteristics:**

   Blue recalls the sky.

   Red reminds one of a tomato.

   Lightness evokes a feather.

6. **Association by resemblance:**

   Journal/review: both are periodical publications and belong to the world of the Press.

   Armchair/sofa: both are used to sit on, and both imply a notion of comfort.

Association is therefore a kind of bridge which:

- sends a new piece of information to be added to a memory that is already stored and

- enables a recollection to come to the surface of our memory.

While in some cases mental associations – whether conscious or subconscious – favour expected, even stereotype answers, (a nail can make one think of a hammer) in many instances established associations are dictated by the social and cultural context and by each individual's attitudes and experience.

The tests in this chapter reflect different aspects of the associative relationship. The section entitled **Indirect Association** contains five tests.

ONE WORD EVOKES ANOTHER

Certain words, through a logical association, evoke others. This test is not scored, but is valuable as training. The aim is not, therefore, to avoid supplying answers which seem obvious.

If, for example, you are asked what words come immediately to mind when you see *feeding-bottle*, you can always show that you have imagination and intelligence by replying: *tractor, tweezers* or *nails!* This is not what is being asked for here. The object of this exercise is to find a logical link, a spontaneous relationship between a new element and a known one.

In the panel opposite you see a list of ten words. You have to write alongside each one the first word you associate with it. It could be that two or three words come immediately to mind. In this case, you will have to make a choice.

You have one minute to find ten associated words. There is no evaluation for this test.

YOUR ANSWERS

	Association
1. *lock*	
2. *sea-plane*	
3. *poppy*	
4. *ramp*	
5. *beehive*	
6. *frequency*	
7. *toreador*	
8. *polish*	
9. *stethoscope*	
10. *ice-axe*	

Answers on page 150

Possible answers

1. barge – river – canal – bargee
2. water – sea
3. flower – drug – opium
4. slope – garage – boatyard
5. bee – honey – swarm – queen
6. radio – waves – often
7. bullfight – bull – Spain
8. shine – slippery – furniture – floor – wax
. doctor – sounding – consultation – check-up
10. mountain – climbing

WE SAID 'FEEDING-BOTTLE'

Of 100 people who were asked the question: when someone says 'feeding-bottle' to you, what word immediately springs to mind?

- 58 people replied *baby*.
- 22 people replied *milk*.
- 17 people replied *nipple*.
- 1 person replied *pram*.
- 1 person replied *cow*.
- 1 person replied *saucepan*.

Taking these results as an example, we can say that 97 per cent of those questioned gave answers that could be considered as the norm. What is the norm? Quite simply, the frequency with which an answer appears.

Answer analysis

1. Several different answers are possible. However, although the suggested words were given spontaneously by the greatest number of people, this does not make them true or correct.

2. If, for a majority of people, the *sea-plane* immediately brings to mind *water*, the reverse of course does not follow. In fact the associative links with the word *water* will more strongly evoke words such as *swimming, holidays, fishing or pollution*. The same goes for all the words in the list. *Furniture*, for example, does not make one think immediately of *polish*.

Remember

To train your memory through associations:

*   Train daily to set up the automatic recall of a word, a thought, an image or a memory working from a fixed point. These association exercises push the memory towards getting a permanent grip on knowledge. They allow knowledge to be brought to the front of the mind and maintained in a state of readiness.

*   You must distinguish between three different steps:

    The logical step. This consists of finding a logical route, starting from a fixed point. Examples: *bread* and *butter, knife* and *fork, train* and *station* . . .

    The cultural step. This uses acquired knowledge. Thus: *Romeo – Juliet, Freud – dreams, Fleming – penicillin* . . .

    The creative step. This is based entirely on your own imagination and is therefore dictated by each individual's psychic life. It is impossible to give examples since you will have your personal associations.

INDIRECT ASSOCIATION

Association sometimes works by stages or successive steps which enable us to pass from one idea to another. Let us take an example: cow/custard. Here there is no immediate connection between, on the one hand, the animal and, on the other hand, the sauce. To link these words, we have to establish a transition between the two. In this case, the intermediate word could be milk. In other words:

cow .... custard

cow – milk – custard

Our thoughts bounce on stepping stones from one point to another. This requires intermediate words to provide a link between two ideas

The aim of the tests that follow is to link up – using one, two, three or four intermediate stages – the words given in the two lists below. Because of the subjective nature of the exercise, there is no scoring.

Test I

Find the intermediate words linking each of the ten words in the left-hand column with the ten words opposite them in the right-hand column. Write the connecting words in the middle column of the answer panel below.

YOUR ANSWERS

1.	boat	....	harmonica
2.	rug	....	pullover
3.	baton	....	festival
4.	cask	....	glass
5.	make-up	....	antiquity
6.	hammer	....	cupboard
7.	bear	....	child
8.	coat	....	book
9.	hair	....	needle
10.	trumpet	....	tyre

Answers on page 154.

Possible answers

It is quite obvious that in a test of this kind not everyone is going to give the same intermediate words. The following answers should therefore only be considered as suggestions. There can, of course, be other possibilities.

1.	boat	*sailor*	harmonica
2.	rug	*wool*	pullover
3.	baton	*band*	festival
4.	cask	*wine*	glass
5.	make-up	*women*	antiquity
6.	hammer	*nails*	cupboard
7.	bear	*teddy-bear*	child
8.	coat	*pocket*	book
9.	hair	*pin*	needle
10.	trumpet	*valve*	tyre

Answer analysis

1. *Sailor* is justified by the fact that on boats many of them play the harmonica.

2. *Wool* is the intermediate word between rug and pullover, since the material is used in making both items.

3. A *band* is led by a conductor who uses a baton to direct the musicians during a festival, for example.

4. *Wine* is originally stored in a cask before it finally arrives in a glass.

5. *Women* were already using make-up in antiquity.

6. *Nails* are driven in with a hammer to fix together the panels in the construction of a cupboard.

7. *Teddy-bear* is the soft toy version of the bear and much loved by a child.

8. A coat normally contains an inside *pocket* into which one can slip a small book.

9. A *hair-pin* is used to secure hair and a needle, like a pin, is used in sewing.

10. You play the right note on a trumpet by pressing down a *valve,* which also controls the air in a tyre.

Test II

The test that follows is similar to the previous one. However, this one is more difficult because the intermediate words are sometimes to be found from a play on the two that are given.

First cover up the suggested possible answers in the panel opposite, then look at the two lists of words in the panel below and in the middle column write the words that provide the link between them.

YOUR ANSWERS

1.	flag	....	painter
2.	door	....	indigestion
3.	fish	....	gate
4.	oak	....	bladder
5.	decanter	....	bathroom
6.	boxer	....	ham
7.	canon	....	make-up
8.	architect	....	bird
9.	school	....	cricket
10.	pet	....	fire

Answers on page 157.

Possible answers

The answers given below are not, of course, definitive. There will be other possibilities and you will not be wrong if you have come up with alternatives, provided there is a genuine link.

1.	flag	*canvas*	painter
2.	door	*bolt*	indigestion
3.	fish	*gudgeon*	gate
4.	oak	*gall*	bladder
5.	decanter	*glass*	bathroom
6.	boxer	*knuckle*	ham
7.	canon	*powder*	make-up
8.	architect	*wren*	bird
9.	school	*test*	cricket
10.	pet	*dog*	fire

Answer analysis

The answers given above were arrived at using a certain logic, but they are far from being the only possible links.

1. Flags can be made of *canvas*, a material commonly used by painters.

2. Doors are kept secure by the use of a *bolt*. One obvious cause of indigestion is when you 'bolt' your food.

3. *Gudgeon* is a freshwater fish, but also a part of a gate hinge.

4. *Galls* are found on oak trees, and indeed are also known as oak-apples. The gall bladder is an internal organ of the body.

5. Decanters are normally made of *glass*, which is also a word for a mirror, very often found in a bathroom.

6. A boxer uses his *knuckles* for hitting his opponent. The word also refers to a tasty joint of ham.

7. In the olden days, *powder* was used to fire off canons. It is also a key element in a woman's make-up.

8. One of the most celebrated of British architects was Sir Christopher *Wren,* which also happens to be the name of one of Britain's most loved species of bird.

9. One of the more onerous duties at school is the sitting of *tests*. The word is also used to describe international cricket matches.

10. Arguably the most popular household pet is the *dog*. And 'fire-dogs' are used to support burning logs on an open fire.

Test III

Now we start moving into top gear. Here you are not required to find just one intermediate word providing an associative link, but to think of two words that provide a logical 'path' between the two given.

Reading from left to right, insert the link words you have found in the two middle columns.

YOUR ANSWERS

1.	rat	....	....	cork
2.	foot	....	....	abattoir
3.	cat	....	....	wall
4.	feather	....	....	lamp
5.	sky	....	....	news
6.	king	....	....	library
7.	door	....	....	journey
8.	flower	....	....	tan
9.	guitar	....	....	postman
10.	fish	....	....	oar

Answers on page 160.

Possible answers

As in the previous test, the answers suggested here are by no means definitive.

1.	rat	*cellar*	*wine*	cork
2.	foot	*shoe*	*leather*	abattoir
3.	cat	*mouse*	*hole*	wall
4.	feather	*bird*	*power-line*	lamp
5.	sky	*storm*	*flash*	news
6.	king	*page*	*book*	library
7.	door	*handle*	*suitcase*	journey
8.	flower	*garden*	*bench*	tan
9.	guitar	*string*	*parcel*	postman
10.	fish	*river*	*rowing-boat*	oar

Answer analysis

The answers given here provide just one path between the first and last words; there are others.

1. The rat is a rodent well-known to frequent the *cellar*, where, among other things, one keeps bottles of *wine* which are sealed with corks.

2. On the foot one wears a *shoe*, often made of *leather*, a by-product of the skins collected at the abattoir.

3. The cat leaps to catch the *mouse* which escapes through a *hole* in the wall.

4. The link between 'feather' and 'lamp' is not perhaps immediately obvious. The feather is found on the *bird* which spends some of its time perched on the power-line taking the electricity into the house to power the *lamp*.

5. When the sky is cloudy and overcast there may be a *storm* and perhaps a *flash* of lightning, which is also the word used for an important news bulletin.

6. The king is attended by a *page,* which also makes up a *book* whose home is in a library.

7. One opens a door using the *handle*, which one also needs to carry a *suitcase* when one goes off on a journey.

8. The flower grows in the *garden* which also has a *bench* on which one stretches out under the sun to get a tan.

9. To get a note from a guitar one plucks a *string*, which is also used to tie up a *parcel* delivered by the postman.

10. Fish live in the *river* which is also where you might use a *rowing-boat* which needs to be propelled using an oar – or preferably two.

Test IV

Our route, by association from one word to the next, is becoming more complex. To reach the final word in the column on the far right, you now have to find three linking words. One idea brings to mind another and each provides an additional link in the chain so that you can find your way from the first word to the last.

First visualise in your mind an image that each word represents. It is not the word that you have to struggle to find, but more the picture it conjures up, which can then be converted into a possible link word.

In the first test of word associations there was, for example, a link to be found between 'boat' and 'harmonica'. To provide an answer, which would be subjective and personal to each individual, there was no need to scour the pages of your mental dictionary to find a word you thought suitable to fill the hole. You just had to imagine a scene in which a sailor on the beach next to a boat was playing his harmonica to pass away the time.

This test is not concerned with solving riddles, nor with any intellectual exercise in word derivation or definition. Put your imagination to work on your personal experience of the everyday world and let it create a chain of words that is logical for you.

Find three intermediate words that provide a link between the first and last and write them in the spaces provided in the centre three columns.

YOUR ANSWERS

1.	tooth	....	....	....	furniture
2.	bishop	....	....	....	snob
3.	map	....	....	....	sleep
4.	cat	....	....	....	cow
5.	razor	....	....	....	match
6.	climber	....	....	....	ruler
7.	bird	....	....	....	paper
8.	town	....	....	....	chalk
9.	sky	....	....	....	orchestra
10.	banns	....	....	....	muscle

Answers on page 164.

Possible Answers

1.	tooth	*saw*	*tree*	*timber*	furniture
2.	bishop	*chess*	*diagonal*	*strut*	snob
3.	map	*itinerary*	*holiday*	*rest*	sleep
4.	cat	*mouse*	*cheese*	*milk*	cow
5.	razor	*cut*	*power*	*candle*	match
6.	climber	*mountain*	*summit*	*politician*	ruler
7.	bird	*plume*	*pen*	*ink*	paper
8.	town	*pavement*	*child*	*hopscotch*	chalk
9.	sky	*star*	*dancer*	*music*	orchestra
10.	banns	*marriage*	*alliance*	*strength*	muscle

Answer analysis

1. A tooth can be found not only in the mouth but also as part of the cutting edge of a *saw*. A saw is used to cut down a *tree*, the *timber* from which is used to make furniture.

2. A bishop is not only a man of the church but also a piece in the game of *chess*, which can only move along the *diagonal*. The diagonal position provides a common means of support, using a *strut*, for example. A person who struts around often gives the impression of being a snob.

3. You use a map to work out the *itinerary* for your *holiday*, an objective of which is to get some *rest*. And the most effective form of rest is sleep.

4. The cat chases the *mouse*, who eats the *cheese*, which is made out of *milk* produced by the cow.

5. The danger of a razor is that it can cause a *cut*. This word is also associated with failure of *power*, which often requires one to light a *candle* using a match.

6. A climber enjoys scaling the *mountain* as far as the *summit*. This is also the word used for a top-level meeting between the chief *politicians* of the world's major countries, who are their rulers.

7. A bird's plumage is made of feathers – or *plumes* – used in former times as *pens* which were dipped in *ink* in order to write on paper.

8. A town street has a *pavement* where you may come across a *child* playing *hopscotch* with the boxes marked out in chalk.

9. When you look at the night sky, you sees *stars*, a word you could also use for famous *dancers*, who inevitably need *music* provided by an orchestra.

10. The banns are read out before a *marriage*, which is a form of *alliance*. An alliance is often made to increase *strength*, something that is also associated with the muscle.

Test V

The final test in this series consists of finding no less than four link words.

It may at first seem that this exercise, with its long route of missing words to connect the two you are given must present serious problems. It does not.

Taking into account the number of words you have to find, think about making the links from right to left as well as from left to right, as an alternative method of reaching a solution.

Example

arrow   ....   lead

An arrow makes one think of a bow, one type of which is the crossbow. Working from the other end, imagine what lead is used for – making windows. And where does one often find leaded windows? In a church. There is, of course, no need to spell out the link between church and cross!

Writing the four connecting words in the middle columns, you would have:

arrow   *bow*   *cross*   *church*   *window*   lead

YOUR ANSWERS

1.	bell	....	....	....	....	skiing
2.	key	....	....	....	....	cinema
3.	step	....	....	....	....	public
4.	winter	....	....	....	....	memory
5.	shoe	....	....	....	....	win
6.	scissors	....	....	....	....	cloud
7.	lighter	....	....	....	....	lemon
8.	parquet	....	....	....	....	game
9.	electricity	....	....	....	....	money
10.	detective	....	....	....	....	destiny

Answers on page 176.

Remember

To find connecting words:

- Do not hesitate to play with homonyms (*rain, rein, reign*) to free up your thought processes in order to reach the final word in the chain.

- Look at all the possible meanings of words and convert them into images in order to create links.

- To practise this type of association exercise and to create an associated network or link without any difficulty, it will help to memorise the first and last words of the chain. Then it is best to close your eyes, concentrate and make up a scenario.

Possible answers

1.	bell	*cow*	*pasture*	*mountain*	*snow*	skiing
2.	key	*ring*	*wedding*	*photograph*	*film*	cinema
3.	step	*platform*	*speaker*	*applause*	*audience*	public
4.	winter	*damp*	*cold*	*handkerchief*	*knot*	memory
5.	shoe	*horse*	*course*	*race*	*gamble*	win
6.	scissors	*hairdresser*	*perm*	*pools*	*rain*	cloud
7.	lighter	*cigarette*	*filter*	*water*	*tonic*	lemon
8.	parquet	*floor*	*error*	*penalty*	*player*	game
9.	electricity	*bulb*	*tulip*	*Dutch*	*round*	money
10.	detective	*story*	*Holmes*	*garden*	*path*	destiny

Answer analysis

1. A bell is hung round the neck of the *cow* that grazes on the *pasture* at the foot of the *mountain*, the top of which is covered with *snow* and therefore ideal for skiing.

2. The best place to keep a key safe is on a *ring*, which is also needed for a *wedding*. Here, of course, there will be plenty of *photographs* taken – and plenty of reels of *film*. And films are shown at the cinema.

3. Steps are needed to climb up on to the *platform*, where the *speaker* receives warm *applause* from an *audience* made up of members of the public.

4. In winter the weather is very often *damp*, which can lead you to catch a *cold*. To blow your nose you will need a *handkerchief*. And you might also use it with a *knot* tied in it, to help jog your memory about something important.

5. Shoes are worn by *horses*, which are often ridden on a *course*. Each *race* is followed by enthusiasts who have a *gamble* in the hope that their horse will win.

6. Scissors are used by the *hairdresser*, who may also give his female customers a *perm*. This word – as an abbreviation of permutation – is also used for special selections on the football *pools*. Another type of pool is formed by the *rain*, which is carried by a cloud.

7. A lighter is used to light a *cigarette*, many of which have a *filter* tip. A filter is also used to purify *water*. One pleasant effervescent drink is called *tonic* water, which is often served with a slice of lemon.

8. Parquet is a type of wood-block *floor*. This has the same sound as 'flaw', which can mean *'error'*. Committing one can result in a *penalty* for the *player* concerned during the course of a game.

9. Electricity provides light via a *bulb*. A common garden bulb is the *tulip*, the best-known being *Dutch* in origin. The expression 'to go Dutch' means 'to pay for yourself' and not 'stand the *round*' because you don't have enough money to pay for everyone.

10. When you think of detective, you might well think of a detective *story*. One of the most celebrated fictional detectives was Sherlock *Holmes*. His names sounds like homes, many of which have a *garden*. In the garden there is almost certainly a *path*, which you may pursue to your destiny.

WHEN A SYLLABLE EVOKES A WORD

This test is more like a game. The object is to find as many words as you can that either start or end with a given syllable.

Example

- Let's take the starting syllable *'cha'*:
  - chariot
  - chagrin
  - chapel
  - chasing

- Let's take the ending syllable *'go'*:
  - cargo
  - Congo
  - embargo
  - tango

There are so many possible answers that this test is not scored. It uses the technique of association and its purpose is to develop and activate your memory.

You have six minutes to complete the two lists of ten words in the table opposite.

YOUR ANSWERS

	Starting syllable CRA *example:* craven	**Ending syllable KET** *example:* bucket
1.		
2.		
3.		
4.		
5.		
6.		
7.		
8.		
9.		
10.		

Answers on page 172

Possible Answers

A   Words with **CRA** as the starting syllable:

1. cracker
2. crackle
3. cradle
4. craning
5. cranium
6. crater
7. cravat
8. craving
9. crayon
10. crazy

B   Words with **KET** as the ending syllable:

1. basket
2. cricket
3. locket
4. market
5. packet
6. racket
7. rocket
8. socket
9. ticket
10. trinket

Answer analysis

1. This test is like the children's game in which you have to use the final syllable of one word as the first syllable of the next. The link is phonetic.

Example: winter – terminal – algebra – bravado – dozen – zenith.

2. This test helps you to think by association and at the same time enables you to dig down and bring out those words that are stored deep in your memory. It reactivates a passive knowledge and encourages you to remember words, even if the meaning of some of them escapes you!

3. Interestingly enough, there are not that many words beginning with **CRA** or ending in **KET**, although in the case of the latter the words we do have are generally very common ones.

A few suggestions

A. Find, in three minutes, ten words that start with each of the following syllables:

- ant

- pro

- tri

- pre

- for

B. Find, in three minutes, ten words that end with each of the following syllables:

- ple

- ter

- tion

- ger

- ral

To achieve the best results without difficulty and in record time, all you have to do is clear your head and concentrate, regarding the chosen syllables as bait to attract the necessary words, regardless of their length or meaning.

Remember

To find a word from a syllable:

- The syllable, whether the first or last of the word, must act as a starting handle to activate your memory's motor. Despite the fact that this exercise looks like just a game, it does have a serious purpose – to train and develop the technique of association. Try these tests out on yourself and your friends.

BETWEEN THE GUITAR AND THE BUTTERFLY

This test consists of looking very closely at the 12 images in the panel that follows, and finding every association that comes to mind. While there is an obvious and logical connection between some of the items, there are also those that may have a subjective relationship. It is all a question of each individual's vision and trains of thought.

The complexity of the network of associations which is one of the memory's main mechanisms is all too evident. The images shown here can be classified in a variety of ways.

- by family

- by resemblance

- by complementarity

This list is by no means exhaustive.

Limit yourself to ten groupings with the aim of fitting as many of the items as you can into each of them. You can put the same items into more than one group.

Example

Let's take five words - *house, fireplace, stone, guard, dog.* You could make the following links:

- dog –guard
- house – fireplace – guard

- house – stone

- dog – house

- dog – fireplace – house

Since this test can be subject to different interpretations, there is no scoring.

You can continue to look at the 12 images while you write the ten linkings that come immediately to mind in the spaces provided. You have three minutes to complete the test.

YOUR ANSWERS

	Possible groupings
1.	
2.	
3.	
4.	
5.	
6.	
7.	
8.	
9.	
10.	

Answers on page 178.

Possible answers

1. guitar – note – flute
2. glass – aquarium – jug
3. mouse – spider – insect – fish – butterfly
4. mouse – cheese
5. spider – insect – butterfly
6. fish – aquarium
7. guitar – flute
8. glass – jug
9. flute – cheese
10. fish – cheese

Answer analysis

1. Among other possible groupings, you could have for example:

   butterfly – insect – spider – mouse

   The reason being that they all have legs.

2. *Flute* and *cheese* have been grouped together in Answer 9 because they both have holes.

3. Answers 1 and 7 are different. The *guitar*, the *note* and the *flute* all belong to the world of music. The *guitar* and the *flute* are both musical instruments.

4. The connections between *mouse* and *cheese, glass* and *jug* or *fish* and *aquarium* are clearly logical. On the other hand, *flute* and *fish* or *glass* and *guitar* would not appear to have any obvious link. However, both groupings do

in fact have something in common which provides perfect justification for associating them. The first pair both begin with the letter 'f' and the second pair with the letter 'g'.

Remember

To make a link between elements:

- Do not hesitate to use associations which come to mind immediately. But don't leave it at that. Read through the list twice, three times. When it comes to building links, there is not just one right answer.

- Each element, be it a word, a drawing or a situation, is part of a network with a multitude of connections and linkages which do not always appear obvious at first sight.

The search for logical connections, just like that for more obscure associations, provides an ideal stepping-off point for stimulating, activating and training your memory.

CHAPTER VI

ATTENTION

& Concentration

In order to develop and improve our memory, we simply have to develop our attention and concentration.

Most of the time, when we are doing a job, our mind is on other things. We cannot remember, when reading, if we were thinking about the car or, when driving, if we were thinking about the dog or, when stroking the dog, whether we were thinking about work – while at work we only think about the holidays!

Attention and concentration are the mainstays of the memory. They are not only its tools but also its supports. But neither is inborn. We have to learn how to develop them.

The tests that follow in the chapter are geared to attention and concentration, the two great assistants of the memory.

READ TO RETAIN

This test requires all your attention. It consists of reading – at your normal speed without getting faster or slower – the following extract from *Jamaica Inn* by Daphne du Maurier.

Then turn to the table on page 184 and answer the ten questions without looking at the text or the answers!

You have two minues to read the extract, which should allow you to run through it twice. Score two points for each correct answer.

Extract

> The squire looked from one to the other in suspicion.
>
> "What about you, Mrs Merlyn? Don't you know where your husband keeps his keys?"
>
> Aunt Patience shook her head. The squire snorted and turned on his heel. "Well, that's easily settled," he said. "We'll have the door down in no time." And he went out into the yard to call his servant. Mary patted her aunt's hand, and drew her close.
>
> "Try not to tremble so," she whispered fiercely. "Anyone can see you have something to hide. Your only chance is to pretend you don't mind, and that he can see anything in the house for all you care."
>
> In a few minutes Mr Bassat returned with the man Richards, who, grinning all over his face at the thought of destruction, carried an old bar he had found in the stable, and which he evidently intended using as a battering ram.
>
> If it had not been for her aunt, Mary would have given herself up to events with some enjoyment. For the first time she would be permitted a view of the barred room. The fact that her aunt, and she too for that matter, would be implicated in any discovery that was made, caused her mixed feelings, however, and for the first time she realised that it was going to be a very difficult task to prove their complete and thorough innocence. No one was likely to believe protestations, with Aunt Patience fighting blindly on the landlord's side.
>
> It was with some excitement, then, that Mary watched Mr Bassat

and his servant seize the bar between them and ram it against the lock of the door. For a few minutes it withstood them, and the sound of the blows echoed through the house. Then there was a splitting of wood and a crash, and the door gave way before them. Aunt Patience uttered a little cry of distress, and the squire pushed past her into the room. Richards leant on the bar, wiping the sweat from his forehead, and Mary could see through to the room over his shoulder. It was dark, of course; the barred windows with their lining of sack kept the light from penetrating the room.

Daphne du Maurier, *Jamaica Inn*

YOUR ANSWERS

	Answers	Score
1. *What is the squire's name?*	M Bassat	·2
2. *What was he looking for?*		
3. *What is the servant's name?*	Richal	2
4. *What was used to break down the door?*	old motal baal	2
5. *Where was it found?*	in barn?	·1
6. *Who went into the room first?*	Squire	2
7. *What was Aunt Patience's surname?*	Merlin	·1
8. *Had Mary been in the room before?*	No	2
9. *What was lining the barred windows?*	Hessi Cloth	·1
10. *Whose side was Aunt Patience fighting on?*	Landlords	2
Total (out of 20)		15

Answers on page 185

Answers for evaluation

1. Bassat
2. The keys
3. Richards
4. An old bar
5. In the stable
6. The squire
7. Merlyn
8. No
9. Sack
10. The landlord

Answer analysis

1. The fact that the order of questions does not strictly follow that of the text is deliberate. This makes the test that little bit harder.

2. As you have no doubt already realised, memory cannot work without attention and concentration. Both are particularly important when you read something since, apart from the pleasure you may get from it, you never know what you might need – or be asked – to extract from it afterwards.

ATTEND TO YOUR READING

The text that follows is an extract from *The Rainbow* by D. H. Lawrence. Like the previous one, this test consists of reading the extract attentively and answering the questions.

Through concentration and attention you will master the art of making your reading more efficient. You will then have no difficulty in answering the questions which follow.

You have two minutes to read the extract. Score two points for each correct answer.

Extract

He went to wash himself. Queer little breaks of consciousness seemed to rise and burst like bubbles out of the depths of his stillness.

"It's got to be done," he said as he stooped to take the shirt out of the fender, "it's got to be done, so why balk it?" And as he combed his hair before the mirror on the wall, he retorted to himself, superficially: "The woman's not speechless dumb. She's not clutterin' at the nipple. She's got the right to please herself, and displease whosoever she likes."

This streak of commonsense carried him a little further.

"Did you want anything?" asked Tilly, suddenly appearing, having heard him speak. She stood watching him comb his fair beard. His eyes were calm and uninterrupted.

"Ay," he said, "where have you put the scissors?"

She brought them to him, and stood watching as, chin forward, he trimmed his beard.

"Don't go an' crop yourself as if you was at a shearin' contest," she said, anxiously. He blew the fine-curled hair quickly off his lips.

He put on all clean clothes, folded his stock carefully, and donned his best coat. Then, being ready, as grey twilight was failing, he went across to the orchard to gather the daffodils. The wind was roaring in the apple-trees, the yellow flowers swayed violently up and down, he heard even the fine whisper of their spears as he stooped to break the flattened, brittle stems of the flowers.

"What's to-do?" shouted a friend who met him as he left the garden gate.

"Bit of courtin', like," said Brangwen.

And Tilly, in a great state of trepidation and excitement, let the wind whisk her over the field to the big gate, whence she could watch him go.

He went up the hill and on towards the vicarage, the wind roaring through the hedges, whilst he tried to shelter his bunch of daffodils by his side. He did not think of anything, only knew that the wind was blowing.

Night was falling, the bare trees drummed and whistled. The vicar, he knew, would be in his study, the Polish woman in the kitchen, a comfortable room, with her child. In the darkest of twilight, he went through the gate and down the path where a few daffodils stooped in the wind, and shattered crocuses made a pale, colourless ravel.

D. H. Lawrence, *The Rainbow*

YOUR ANSWERS

		Answers	Score
1.	What did Brangwen take out of the fender?	shirt	
2.	Who suddenly appeared as he was talking to himself?	Tilly	
3.	What did she bring to him?	Scissors	
4.	What part of the day was it?		
5.	Why did Brangwen go to the orchard?	To get flowers?	
6.	Who met him at the garden gate?	friend	
7.	Where was he heading towards?	Vicarage	
8.	What was he thinking about?	Polish 9.8	
9.	Who would be in the kitchen?	Peaaly.	
10.	What time of year was it?	?	
	Total (out of 20)		

Answers on page 190

Answer analysis

1. In a way this test presents less difficulty than the previous one, since the questions are asked in the order in which the detail appears in the extract. Moreover, the previous test was good practice and fixed the rules of the game in your mind.

2. One slightly different angle here is that some of the questions require greater attention to the general description than to particular facts – such as names. And the final question demands some deduction. The fact that the scene takes place in early spring can be deduced from the mention of daffodils and crocuses (obviously springtime), while the trees are still bare (therefore early).

3. You should now know the difference between automatic and attentive reading. People who maintain that they do not remember what they read have most probably not learned to discipline their attention. Obviously one must exclude those problems of memory whose cause is pathological.

Remember

To make your reading active and positive:

- You must discipline your attention. Whether you are reading a book, an article in a newspaper or a prospectus, it is important to do so on the basis that you may well be required to answer some unexpected questions afterwards.

- Never remembering what you have read is rather like losing your glasses or keys. In effect, lack of attention damages the accuracy of our memories.

Answers for evaluation

1. His shirt
2. Tilly
3. Scissors
4. Failing grey twilight
5. To gather daffodils
6. A friend
7. The vicarage
8. Nothing
9. The Polish woman and her child
10. Early spring

ONE WORD HIDES ANOTHER

Concentration requires effort. There are many who fail to fix their minds on a particular subject, an idea or a piece of work.

In order to concentrate, we have to respect a certain discipline in our behaviour. People talking nearby, music playing, the telephone ringing . . . such distractions present major obstacles which we must look on as 'aggressive' towards concentration.

Sometimes we willingly let ourselves be distracted, notably when we are involved in some tedious work. In this case, we have to concentrate on our objectives and persuade ourselves that the end justifies the means.

This simple change of attitude will enable us to put concentration before anything else.

In the list of words overleaf, the letters of each word can be written in a different order to form a new word. This new word can be any part of speech (noun, adjective, adverb, verb, etc.), but you must use all the letters in the first word.

Example: pale = plea, kiss = skis.

You have three minutes to find ten different words from the ones given in the list that follows. Score two points for each correct answer.

Practical tip

To remember someone's name, you could make up an anagram that reflects, say, his business or occupation. For example, you meet a designer called Carter. The ideal anagram would be 'Tracer', since part of his work could involve tracing the outlines or details of images. Or take someone called Mr Shaw who runs a dry cleaning business. The perfect anagram here would be 'Wash'. You can have a lot of fun making up your own, with names of people you come across.

YOUR ANSWERS

	Word found	Score
1. PACE		
2. LACKS		
3. PIER		
4. MARE		
5. SUBTLE		
6. VEER		
7. PEAR		
8. GARDEN		
9. SAINT		
10. EVIL		
	Total (out of 20)	

Answers on page 194

Possible answers for evaluation

1. cape

2. slack

3. ripe

4. ream

5. bustle

6. ever

7. reap

8. danger

9. stain

10. live

Answer analysis

1. When you rearrange the letters of one word in a different order to create another, that word is known as an anagram. Not only do anagrams figure prominently in cryptic crosswords, but they have been regularly used by novelists, particularly satirists, wishing to disguise references and, in some cases, avoid possible libel actions. One famous example is the political satire of Samuel Butler, which he entitled *Erewhon* – that is, Nowhere!

2. For some of the words in this list there are, of course, alternative answers. For example, *saint* could also be *satin* and *evil* could equally be *vile*. For *pear* you could have put *pare* or *rape*. Naturally you should score full points for correct anagrams even if they do not appear in the list of answers given.

3. Even though the words in this list were simple ones,

you may have run out of time searching for alternatives. But do not be put off. If you try again, you will certainly come up with better results. Success in such mental gymnastics depends very much on your attention and concentration, but also on your willingness to invest the time to learn how to strengthen and develop your memory.

4. To make up anagrams, you must not only look at the whole word but also dissect it and rearrange its parts. It is important to play around with the letters, making up different elements and juggling them about, breaking the word apart and leap-frogging letters and syllables. You must look at the word from every possible angle.

Remember

To find other possible words by rearranging the letters of existing ones:

- Concentrate and try to discover all the alternatives as quickly as possible, even those that seem improbable, in order to find one that makes a word.

- Do not persist with just one particular type of combination.

- Clear your mind and let your attention and concentration occupy the space.

HUNT THE ANAGRAM

This test is the same as the last one. It consists of re-arranging the letters of each word in the list to make another word.

You have three minutes to find ten different words. Score two points for each correct answer.

YOUR ANSWERS

	Word found	Score
1. MENTAL		
2. ULTIMATE		
3. REACTION		
4. DRAWER		
5. IGNITED		
6. DEBILE		
7. REGRADED		
8. ERASURES		
9. DENTIST		
10. RECANT		
Total (out of 20)		

Answers on page 198

Possible answers for evaluation

1. lament

2. mutilate

3. creation

4. reward

5. dieting

6. edible

7. regarded

8. reassure

9. stinted

10. nectar

Answer analysis

1. Thanks to the previous test, your brain's mechanism knew how to work to make up anagrams from this list of words. Some were more difficult, others simple but perhaps not immediately obvious.

2. As with the previous test, if you have found other anagrams which do not appear in the list of possible answers, score two points all the same – if they are real words, of course.

3. Particularly with longer words, it is always a good idea to look for obvious groups of letters that make up starting or finishing syllables. Obvious examples here include *re* to begin a word and *ment, ate, tion, ing* and *ed* to end a word. Then it is just a question of rearranging the letters that still remain in order to find your anagram. Of course, such syllables will not always provide a solution, but they do act as a starting point if you cannot 'see' another word immediately.

Remember

To use your attention and concentration as effective tools:

* Do not keep worrying about the time limits given, but rather concentrate entirely on the objective. Probably the most apt quote here is from a nineteenth century French surgeon – one Dominique Larrey – whose main claim to fame is that he took four minutes to perform an amputation. He was quoted as saying: "Since we are in a hurry, let's take our time."

* Read each word quickly from left to right and then right to left. Repeat this, but jump over first one letter and then two in order to find the possible links or anchor points for rearranging the letters to give another word.

THE FLOWER MARKET

Crosswords, like Scrabble or other word games of the same sort, are exercises that can only help maintain a certain part of the memory.

The next test adopts a slightly different approach. You have to find the names of ten flowers hidden in the letter grid. All the letters that make up individual words are adjacent, either to one side or at an angle.

You may find the same word more than once, but you cannot use an individual letter twice for the same word. You can, however, use the same letter more than once if it fits into two different words. Do not be surprised if you don't use all the letters.

You have ten minutes to find and write down the names of the ten flowers. Score two points for each correct answer.

YOUR ANSWERS

	Name of flower	Score
1.		
2.		
3.		
4.		
5.		
6.		
7.		
8.		
9.		
10.		
	Total (out of 20)	

Answers on page 204

Answers for evaluation

1. Pansy

2. Tulip

3. Rose

4. Dahlia

5. Lilac

6. Iris

7. Begonia

8. Delphinium

9. Crocus

10. Daffodil

Answer analysis

All the flowers to be found in this 'market' are common varieties. To make life a little easier, the key was to start in the top left-hand corner of the grid with the letter 'P'. That is not to say, however, that you could not have made a start anywhere.

THE MULTI-COLOURED INK

This test works on the same principle as the last one. The object is always to teach you to move round the information in order to discover an organising principle which will help you to memorise.

You have ten minutes to find and write down the ten colours contained in the grid inside the inkpot pictured on the next page. Score two points for each correct answer.

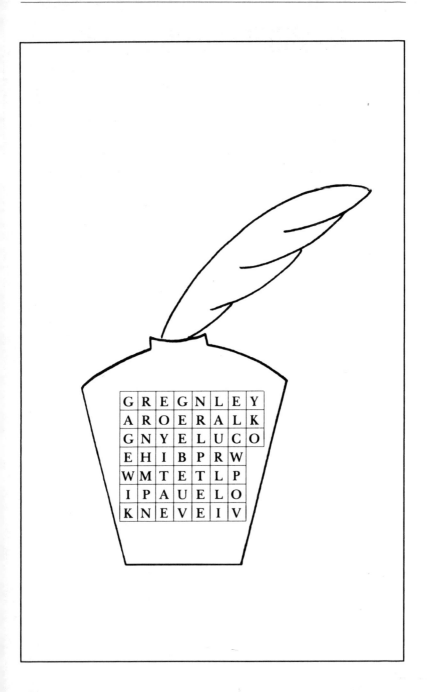

YOUR ANSWERS

	Name of colour	Score
1.		
2.		
3.		
4.		
5.		
6.		
7.		
8.		
9.		
10.		
	Total (out of 20)	

Answers on page 208

Answers for evaluation

1.	Green	6.	Pink
2.	Orange	7.	Black
3.	Grey	8.	Yellow
4.	White	9.	Purple
5.	Mauve	10.	Violet

Answer analysis

As in the previous test, to make things easier you should have started in the top left-hand corner with the letter 'G' for *green*. But you could have started anywhere and still achieved the same result. Incidentally, no letter was used twice in this puzzle.

THE INFERNAL RECTANGLE

This test of attention, like the previous ones, requires organisation. How many rectangles can you count in the grid below?

You have three minutes to answer. Score 20 points for the right answer.

YOUR ANSWER

Number of rectangles	Score

Answer on page 210

Answer for evaluation

36 rectangles

Answer analysis

To come up quickly and easily with the answer to this test, which is based on attention and organisation, you need to fully explore the resources of the diagram. It is therefore best to number each of the rectangles and use these to note all the possibilities.

1	2	3
4	5	6
7	8	9

Thus:

There are 9 small rectangles inside the diagram. Plus the outer rectangle which encloses all of these. This makes 10. There remain 26 others, which should have been noted as follows: 123, 12, 23, 456, 45, 56, 789, 78, 89, 147, 14, 47, 258, 25, 58, 369, 36, 69, 123456, 456789, 124578, 1245, 4578, 235689, 2356, 5689.

This gives you a total of 36.

LETTERS AND DOTS

The two exercises in attention and concentration that follow are very well-known. They involve the development of the right hemisphere of the brain.

1. There are lots of letters in the following grid and it would appear difficult to remember such a long list. However, there is a way of memorising them without having to learn them all.

R	N	N	T	O
O	G	E	H	M
L	S	S	E	O
L	T	G	R	S
I	O	A	N	S

2. Join up the nine dots below using four straight lines without lifting your pencil off the paper and without passing through the same dot twice.

Answers on page 212

Answers

1.   *"Rolling stones gather no moss"*
2.

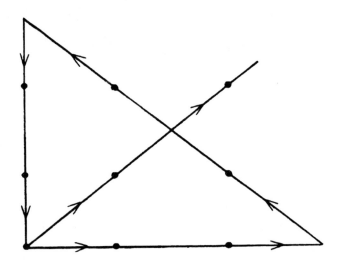

Answer analysis

1.   From a very tender age, we have been taught to read horizontally from left to right. As a matter of cultural habit, there is an automatic tendency to try and tackle the exercise in this way. However, if we read **vertically** down each column starting on the left, we find the letters make up a well-known proverb: *"Rolling stones gather no moss".* This is clearly much easier to remember than the letters which at first glance have no connecting organisation at all.

2.   To enlarge your vision, you must learn how to break free of any preconceived ideas and take a broader view. Then things which seem impossible while your vision is blinkered will become quite clear and simple.

CHAPTER VII

TAKING STOCK
of Your Memory

IN EVERYDAY LIFE

With each of the questions that follow, tick the relevant YES or NO box.

	YES	NO
1. *Are you forever looking for your keys or glasses?*		X
2. *Do you leave the windows open or pans on the cooker when you go out?*		X
3. *Do you regularly forget your telephone number?*		X
4. *Do you often make everyday errors or mistakes through simple oversight?*	X	
5. *Do you frequently leave your belongings (umbrella, bag, coat, etc) in a public place or at friends?*		X
6. *Do you regard yourself as someone who doesn't need to make notes of what you have to do?*		X
7. *Do you regularly arrive late for your meetings?*		X
8. *Do you forget where you have put things at home?*	X	
9. *Do you regularly muddle up days of the week?*	X	
10. *Have you forgotten yesterday's headlines on the television or radio?*	X	
TOTAL	4	6

See page 223

MEMORY AND THE UNCONSIOUS

In *The Psychopathology of Everyday Life,* Freud explains that our missed actions – and so our oversights – are not, in many cases, due either to chance or organic failure. They must be attributed to an action of the unconscious which occurs to upset the functioning of the conscious life.

Such phenomena sometimes appear in a spectacular way. We can, for example, suddenly forget the telephone number of someone we have had an argument with, although we had remembered it for years before then. If we forget the number without there having been any dispute, that surely tells us something!

In the same way, if I miss a meeting with someone – and particularly if I miss several – there is no need to look very far: deep down inside me, I do not want to attend these meetings.

Our failures of memory can thus shed light on ourselves. Tell me what you forget and I will tell you who you are!

THE MEMORY THAT FAILS

What one calls the 'amnesic complaint' does not always really correspond to problems caused by a deficient memory. How can we remember something if it was poorly perceived in the first place? We know that one cannot regard the memory as a marginal function, independent of everything else. It is linked to our brain, to our senses, to our body. One even talks of a genetic memory.

In order to provide the most precise information and to pass it on accurately, our senses must be functioning at an optimum level. If they collect information in a rough and ready way, the message they register will be incomplete. This produces a distortion, a jamming effect that can only result in omissions and errors of a kind that are not true to the initial information.

Before resigning yourself to the idea that you are losing your memory, it is imperative that you check you do not need glasses or that those you are wearing do not need changing. The same goes for your hearing.

It is equally important to note that tobacco, alcohol and drugs affect the sensory faculties. As well as uncontrolled or unpredictable reactions and damage on an organic level, these substances can also result in poor perception and thus bring about problems that one wrongly attributes to a poor memory. In the same way, vitamin deficiency or a bad diet can result in a malfunction of the senses

The brain can be regarded as the memory's HQ. It is the reception office, the principal shop, the temporary or long-term warehouse. It is the receiver, the transmitter and the computer. Its stock of information is not stored haphazardly, since it has to be operational at any given moment.

For all these reasons, it must benefit from the utmost care and not be allowed to deteriorate through an increase in work, fatigue, stress and anxiety.

Fortunately, mental or certain pathological illnesses are not the only causes of poor memory. Nevertheless, you ignore any signs of deterioration in your memory at your peril. It is advisable to seek advice. If the medical diagnosis proves negative, it is imperative that in order to safeguard, look after and develop your memory, you lead a healthy life and put your brain through a suitable exercise routine – gently but daily.

LOSS OF MEMORY LINKED TO OLD AGE

Faced with this problem, one must remain vigilant. It could be an early symptom of one of the degenerative neurological illnesses such as Alzheimer's. There generally follows some difficulty in visual recognition and failures in the functioning of the sufferer's reasoning, speech and movement.

Although these illnesses occur most frequently among old people, one should always be aware that, in every person, neurones die and are not replaced. However, 'normal' ageing allows the neurones that remain – and they exist in sufficient numbers – to take on the work of those that are missing. They create synaptic contacts (joining points between two neurones), but these are made more slowly. Consequently, old age implies slower learning and recall.

For this reason – and in order to put a brake on the acceleration of slowing down – it is important to practise a certain number of exercises that stimulate the memory.

YOUR WAY OF LIFE

With each of the questions that follow, tick the relevant YES or NO box.

	YES	NO
1. *Do you sleep badly or too little?*		X
2. *Are you incessantly on edge?*		X
3. *Do you eat excessively heavy meals, particularly in the evening?*		X
4. *Do you go to bed at irregular times?*		X
5. *Do you not walk during the day except on medical advice?*		X
6. *Do you smoke, drink alcohol or take a lot in the way of stimulants such as tea or coffee?*		X
7. *Do you have trouble relaxing?*		X
8. *Do you like sleeping in an excessively heated bedroom?*		X
9. *Do you take things too much to heart to the point of being permanently preoccupied?*	X	
10. *Do you feel very tired as soon as you wake up?*	?	
TOTAL		

See page 223

YOUR EARLY MEMORIES

With each of the questions that follow, tick the relevant YES or NO box.

	YES	NO
1. *Do you remember your first toy?*	X	
2. *Do you remember the first song you ever learned?*	X	X
3. *Do you remember the first thing you learned to recite by heart?*		X
4. *Do you remember the colour of the walls in your bedroom when you were a child?*	?	X
5. *Do you remember the first animal that frightened you?*	X	
6. *Do you remember the name of your first teacher?*	X	
7. *Do you remember the shape of the first car you ever saw?*		X
8. *Do you remember the reason for your first reprimand?*	?	X
9. *Do you remember your first great fear?*		X
10. *Do you remember the first letter you ever wrote?*		X
TOTAL	3	

See page 223

THE DIFFERENT TYPES OF AMNESIA

1. **Anterograde amnesia** (memories affected: those that date from after the start of the problem)

    Patients forget recent facts. They notice events in the present but do not consciously register them. Current memories exist without the patients knowing how to recall them. However, those affected retain their intellectual faculties. This amnesia, which was identified by Korsakoff in 1889, is especially evident when it comes to new verbal information.

    Causes:

    *   Chronic or prolonged alcoholism, malnutrition, digestive problems.

    *   Tumours: of the base of the brain or frontal lobes.

    *   Vascular cerebral accidents: rupture of the aneurysm (in some cases), amnesic ictus.

    *   Encephalitis: herpetic encephalitis.

    *   Operations: resection of the temporal medial lobe in the case of serious epilepsy.

    It should be noted that a Vitamin B1 deficiency can be found in nearly all the causes of amnesic problems as defined in Korsakoff's Syndrome. Moreover, in certain cases, to avoid a worsening of the situation, patients are injected with this vitamin.

2. **Retrograde amnesia** (memories affected: those that date from before the start of the problem)

    Patients forget facts from their early history. They can no longer recall those memories fixed in the past. These gaps can take different forms. As yet no-one has been able to find a reason for them. Distinction is made here between *lacunary* (incomplete) and *elective amnesia*.

Causes:

- Following a cranial trauma.

- Coming out of a coma.

  These forms of amnesia reveal themselves in patients forgetting their own identity and life history. There are some – albeit very rare – cases of total retrograde amnesia, for the cause of which one would perhaps have to turn to psychiatry. Scientists have not detected any organic cause.

3. **Sensory amnesia**
   This type of amnesia is due to precise cerebral lesions and provokes a loss of automatic co-ordination in the patient's gestures. This is apraxia. It may also cause the loss of automatic co-ordination of sensations and cutaneous or muscular feelings. This is agnosia.

4. **Speech amnesia or aphasia**

   - Localised aphasia (in reception and execution).

   - Deeper aphasia.

5. **Hypermnesia**
   The characteristic here is a capacity for a prodigious memory.

   - Accidental or occasional case.

   - Chronic case, for example with certain mental disorders.

   - Delirium, drug influence, hallucinatory emotional shocks.

6. **Paramnesia**
   Illusions of the memory. Often found with patients suffering from Korsakoff's Syndrome and some epileptics. It reveals itself rather like this:

The patient thinks he recognises a place, a situation . . . believing that they belong to his past, while in fact all is new to him. The patient is mentally confused.

General observation:

- The same cause can provoke several amnesic problems of a different nature.

- One can suffer from amnesic problems following intoxication from lead or carbon monoxide.

THE THREE QUESTIONNAIRES

In everyday life
(see page 214)

If you have answered YES to all ten questions asked here, you lack attention, concentration and organisation. Perhaps, with the appropriate exercises, you will come to train and develop your memory. However, as a precaution, it would better if you went to seek professional advice.

Between six and nine YES answers, you must be very careful and not mistrust such 'slips'. They can hide other things. To reassure yourself, do not hesitate to go and see your doctor.

Your way of life
(see page 218)

If you have answered YES to all ten questions asked here, go and seek professional advice immediately.

Between six and nine YES answers, be conscious of not letting your present state become a habit, because otherwise you are running a number of risks. As a precaution, do not hesitate to go and see your doctor.

Your early memories
(see page 219)

If you have answered YES to all ten questions asked here, that is excellent. Your long-term memory is very efficient. Or perhaps you have parents who kept on repeating these adorable memories!

Between six and nine YES answers, your long-term memory shows no serious lapse. One could even say it is very good.

223

PRACTICAL ADVICE

- Learn to sleep well. Your bedroom should be peaceful, dark and well-ventilated. The temperature should not exceed 18°C, although 15°C would be even better. Avoid beds that are too soft. Place cushions under the mattress in order to sleep with your legs raised.

- Go to bed at a regular time.

- Especially at night, avoid meals that are too heavy, excess alcohol, mixtures of wine and other drinks and, of course, too much tea, coffee and tobacco.

- Make yourself walk at least one hour per day. If you decide to take up a sport or start going to a gym, make sure you are in good health and, if necessary, check first with your doctor.

- Before going to bed, walk for about 20 minutes, relax, have a bath (not too hot, not too cold) or a shower and drink a little herbal tea. You must make sure you do all this to prepare yourself for a relaxing night's sleep.

- Before going to sleep, read a few pages of a book or listen to some restful music. Avoid sleeping with images of a violent film still in your head!

A good healthy life backed up by simple principles, the will to succeed and sound judgement must be the Number One ally for your memory.

Memory does not develop by itself. In someone who lives the life of a vegetable, it has every chance of wilting. On the other hand, an attitude that is receptive and open to the world, inquisitive and active aids its development.

Remember . . . the memory only wears out when it is not being used.

We must end with one fundamental observation. We remember something well if, at the moment we notice it, we already have some idea of its future usefulness.